MICOS:
A MICROPROGRAMMABLE
COMPUTER SIMULATOR

OTHER LANGUAGE BOOKS OF INTEREST FROM COMPUTER SCIENCE PRESS

Wayne Amsbury
Structured Basic and Beyond

William Findlay and David Watt
Pascal: An Introduction to Methodical Programming, Second Edition

Vern McDermott and Diana Fisher
Learning Basic Step by Step, Student Text

Vern McDermott and Diana Fisher
Learning Basic Step by Step, Teacher's Guide

James J. McGregor and Alan H. Watt
Simple Pascal

Ronald H. Perrott and Donald C. S. Allison
PASCAL for FORTRAN Programmers

Gerald N. Pitts and Barry L. Bateman
Essentials of COBOL Programming: A Structured Approach

MICOS:
A MICROPROGRAMMABLE
COMPUTER SIMULATOR

LUBOMIR BIC
University of California, Irvine

COMPUTER SCIENCE PRESS

Computer Science Press, Inc.
11 Taft Court
Rockville, Maryland 20850

1 2 3 4 5 6   88 87 86 85 84

Library of Congress Cataloging in Publication Data

Bic, Lubomir, 1951—
    MICOS: a microprogrammable computer simulator.

    Bibliography: p.
    Includes index.
    1. MICOS (Computer Program)   2. Assembler language
(Computer program language)   3. Digital computer
simulation.   4. Microprogramming.   I. Title.
II. Title: M.I.C.O.S.
QA76.6.B526   1982   001.64'24   82-23627
ISBN 0-914894-76-5

CONTENTS

PREFACE

MICOS, a MIcroprogrammable COmputer Simulator, is a software package developed at the University of California, Irvine, as an instructional tool to teach the basic principles of assembly language and microprogramming.

It provides an *assembler* which allows the student to write programs in a simple assembly language and to translate these into machine language programs. An *interpreter* written in a *microprogramming language* exists which allows the machine language programs to be executed.

The interpreter itself may be extended by writing new sections of microcode which are translated by a *microprogram assembler* and appended to the existing interpreter. Thus, each student has the opportunity to implement his/her own additional instructions at the assembly/machine level interpreted by the new microcode.

INTRODUCTION

Computation in its most general form refers to a process during which a *processor* executes (interprets) a sequence of *instructions* constituting a *program*. This general scheme may be implemented at many different levels of complexity. At one end of the spectrum there are high-level languages such as Pascal, in which each instruction may incorporate a rather complex function, and at the other end there are programming languages in which the power of an instruction does not go beyond the opening of hardware gates, causing values to flow from one register to another. In accordance with the complexity of a programming language is the complexity of the underlying processor (interpreter), ranging from a very large software system (the interpreter for the language) to a simple set of hardware circuits.

In addition to the degree of complexity, another characteristic distinguishing programming languages may be considered. For any computation there are two general schemes for carrying out the task specified by a program:

a) direct *interpretation,* or
b) *translation* with subsequent interpretation

A program is said to be interpreted if there exists a processor (the interpreter) capable of fetching and directly executing instructions of the language in which the program is written.

A program is said to be translated if there exists a program (the translator) which is capable of translating the program into another (executable) language. For this new language there must exist a processor (interpreter) capable of executing the program.

In the MICOS system we are concerned with four distinct languages (refer to figure 1). The following discussion is intended to indicate the "flavor" of each of these languages.

At the highest level there is the *assembly-level programming language* (assembly language for short) used by the application programmer, i.e., the user of the MICOS system. This language utilizes mnemonic names to facilitate the task of program development. An example of a MICOS assembly language instruction is BR M which causes the program to "branch" to the label M, causing execution to continue with the instruction labeled M. The complete instruction set of the assembly language will be presented in chapter 2.

Before an assembly language program can be executed it must be translated into a corresponding program in *machine language,* since there is no processor able to interpret the symbolic names directly. Each mnemonic operation code and the corresponding (symbolic) operand are translated into numeric values. Hence, the entire machine instruction (corresponding to exactly one assembly language instruction) is represented as a sequence of zeros and ones. Because of the MICOS architecture, 24 bits (*bi*nary *d*igits) are used for each instruction. An example of a machine language instruction is the sequence: 0000 0000 0011 0000 0010 0001.

Chapter 3 discusses the formats of machine language instructions and illustrates how assembly language programs are translated into machine language programs.

In order to improve the readability of machine language instructions, the hexadecimal number representation shall be used frequently throughout this handbook. For example, the hexadecimal equivalent of the above instruction is the sequence 003021. (Appendix F contains an introduction to number systems.)

A program translated into machine language may be executed by a processor called the *MICOS interpreter.* For the assembly language programmer, the internal functioning of this processor is of no interest. It could be implemented as a collection of hardware circuits, each capable of executing one machine instruction; it could also be implemented as a program—a collection of software routines capable of executing these instructions. The MICOS processor is implemented using the latter scheme. Such processors are referred to as *microprogrammed* (as opposed to hardwired—implemented as hardware circuits).

The language in which the interpreter is written is called the *symbolic microprogramming language.* It comprises nine instructions, each of which consists of a mnemonic operation code and symbolic operands. An example of a symbolic microprogramming instruction is ADD X,AUX,MDR, which adds the contents of the registers X and AUX transfering the result to the register MDR.

Chapter 5 presents the complete instruction set of the microprogramming language.

Before the interpreter may be employed to execute machine language programs, it must itself be translated into an executable program. This program is composed of instructions from the *numeric microprogramming language.* This language is the lowest in the hierarchy and is executed at the hardware level, that is, the processor for the numeric microprogramming language is implemented as a collection of hardware circuits. An example of a numeric microprogramming instruction is the sequence 0110 0001 0011 0000 0001 1010. The formats of these instructions will be discussed in chapter 6.

Figure 1 on the following page summarizes the complete language and execution hierarchy of the MICOS system.

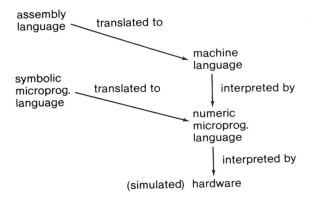

Figure 1.

PART I

Assembly Language Programming

Chapter 1

BASIC ORGANIZATION OF THE ASSEMBLY LANGUAGE LEVEL

1.1 ARCHITECTURE OVERVIEW

From the point of view of the assembly language programmer, MICOS can be considered to consist of the following three major components (figure 1.1):

- A *memory* comprising 512 words with a word length of 24 bits. The memory is capable of holding a machine language program to be executed and a data structure called a stack, used by the program (see section 1.2).
- A *processor* capable of executing the program stored in memory. The detailed implementation of the processor is the topic of Part II of this handbook—in Part I we only describe the functions of the processor as seen by the assembly language programmer.
- An *input/output interface* capable of communicating data values between the user and the program under execution. These are input values supplied to the program for processing and output values returned from the program as the results of computation. All input values are supplied to the I/O interface as a collection of data referred to as the *input file*. Similarly, all results are returned in the form of an *output file*. (The details of input and output are discussed in section 2.9.)

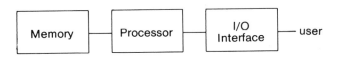

Figure 1.1

1.2 MEMORY ORGANIZATION

The memory of MICOS is capable of holding only one program at a time. Each program consists of a sequence of machine language instructions and data constants. The program is stored in memory starting at location 0 (figure 1.2). Each instruction or data constant occupies exactly one memory word (24 bits).

Note: Throughout this handbook the terms 'memory *word*' and 'memory *location*' will be used as synonyms. Similarly, the terms '*location number*' will be sometimes referred to as the '*address*' of that location.
Figure 1.2 illustrates the basic memory organization.

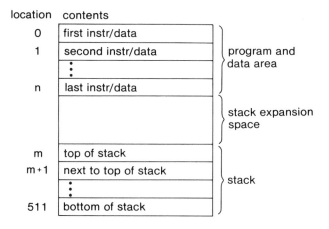

Figure 1.2

The operation of the MICOS system is stack-oriented, which means that most instructions (e.g., all arithmetic and logical instructions) accept their operands from and return their results to a data structure called a *stack*. A stack is a (possibly empty) sequence of values, access to which is limited by the following restriction: new values may be added to, or existing values removed from, only one end of the stack, called the *top of the stack* (*tos*). Thus, the value placed on the stack first (the bottom of the stack) will be removed last. In MICOS, the stack is kept in memory starting at the highest location (511) which becomes the bottom of the stack. Initially, the stack is empty. As execution progresses, values may be added to the stack causing the stack to grow toward the program stored in the upper portion of the memory.

The operation of adding a value to the stack is usually referred to as *pushing* a value on the stack. Similarly, values may be removed, causing the stack to shrink. This operation is usually referred to as *popping* a value from the stack.

Chapter 2

ASSEMBLY LANGUAGE PROGRAMMING

The purpose of this chapter is to present the complete assembly language instruction set and to illustrate the function of individual instructions using small programming examples.

Each assembly language instruction is characterized by an *operation code* (opcode for short) which specifies the operation to be performed. Each opcode, e.g. LDI, is an acronym of the corresponding instruction name, e.g. *load i*mmediate.

Depending on the instruction type, the opcode may be followed by an *operand* field consisting of a data constant or a memory address specification. Instructions which require an operand will be referred to as *one-operand instructions*; instructions consisting of only the opcode will be referred to as *zero-operand instructions*.

2.1 LOADING AND STORING THE TOP-OF-STACK VALUE

The following three instructions, LDI, LOAD, and STORE, have in common the function of moving a value to or from the top of the stack. They are used for the loading of operands required by subsequent operations on the stack, and for the storing of results produced during computation into memory locations.

```
LDI c (load immediate)
```

   This instruction causes the constant c, supplied as the operand, to be pushed on top of the stack, thus increasing the length of the stack by one.

   The constant c may be an integer value between -2048 and $+2047$. Any number outside of this range will result in an error, causing the program execution to be aborted. This restriction is imposed by the underlying machine instruction format, as will be discussed in chapter 3.

Example 2.1   The instruction LDI 5 causes the constant value 5 to be pushed on the stack and thus become the current top-of-stack (tos). Figure 2.1 shows the stack before and after execution of this instruction.

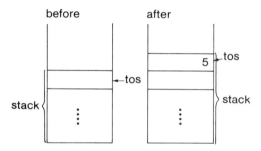

Figure 2.1

   This instruction causes the contents of memory location M to be copied and pushed on top of the stack. The length of the stack is thereby increased by one, while the contents of location M remain unchanged.

   The value M must be an integer between 0 and 511, which is the range of existing memory locations. Any value outside of this range will result in an error, causing the computation to be aborted.

Example 2.2   Assume that memory location 5 now contains the value 256. (In section 2.6 it is explained how values may be placed into desired memory locations.) Figure 2.2 then shows the effect of executing the instruction LOAD 5: a copy of the contents of location 5 is pushed on the stack while the location 5 itself remains unchanged.

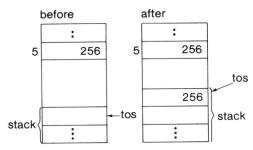

Figure 2.2

Note the essential difference between the instructions LDI and LOAD. In the first case the operand is supplied immediately as part of the instruction, while in the second case only the location of the operand is specified. (See also section 2.10 on addressing modes.)

STORE M

This instruction causes the current top-of-stack value to be transferred to memory location M. The previous content of location M is overwritten with the new value, and the length of the stack is decreased by one since the current top-of-stack value is to be discarded.

It should be noted that the top-of-stack value is not actually erased from memory when the stack pointer is moved. It still remains in the same place, however, there is no way to access that value with any subsequent stack operation. It will be overwritten by the next value pushed on the stack.

Example 2.3 Assume that the current top-of-stack (tos) value is 25. Figure 2.3 shows the effect of executing the instruction STORE 7: The value 25 is stored in location 7 and the stack length is decreased. The value 25 which remained above the new top-of-stack value will be overwritten when the stack "grows" as a result of any subsequent push operations.

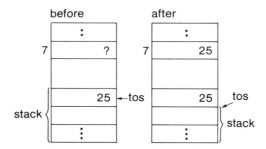

Figure 2.3

2.2 ARITHMETIC INSTRUCTIONS

In the MICOS assembly language all arithmetic instructions use the current top-of-stack values as their operands, thus the operand field of the instruction must remain blank. If this is not the case, the assembler will report an error.

The following two instructions perform the addition and subtraction operations on the two top-most values of the stack respectively.

```
ADD
```

This instruction removes the two top-most values from the stack and replaces them with their sum.

Example 2.4   Assume that the two top-most values of the stack are 25 and 1. Figure 2.4 then demonstrates the effect of the instruction ADD by showing the stack before and after execution of that instruction.

```
SUB
```

This instruction removes the two top-most values from the stack and replaces them with their difference, such that the top-most value is subtracted from the value below.

Figure 2.4

Example 2.5   Write a section of code that subtracts the contents of locations 11 and 12 from the content of location 10:

```
LOAD 10
LOAD 11
SUB
LOAD 12
SUB
```

To illustrate the function of the above code, assume that locations 10, 11, and 12 contain the values 5, 4, and 3, respectively. Figure 2.5 then shows the contents of the stack after execution of each of the above instructions.

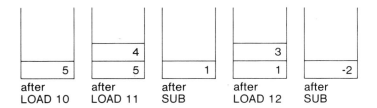

Figure 2.5

Any memory location can hold integer values in the range from -8388608 to $+8388607$. This restriction is imposed by the 24-bit length of each memory word as will be discussed in chapter 3. An ADD or SUB instruction may, deliberately or by mistake, attempt to violate this restriction by adding/subtracting numbers which produce results outside of the above range. Any such attempt will result in an error causing the computation to be aborted.

2.3 BRANCH INSTRUCTIONS

In order to allow the programmer to alter the sequential flow of control, the assembly language provides four branch instructions — one unconditional and three conditionals:

```
BR M (branch)
```

This instruction causes an unconditional branch to the specified memory location M; the next instruction executed after BR is the instruction in the memory location M.

As with the instructions LOAD and STORE, the memory address M must lie within the range of legal memory locations (0-511).

```
BZE M (branch on zero)
BPL M (branch on plus or zero)
BMI M (branch on minus)
```

Each of the above instructions causes a conditional branch to the specified location M. The branch is performed only if the current top-of-stack value satisfies the respective condition, i.e., it must be equal to zero in the case of BZE, it must be non-negative (greater than or equal to zero) in the case of BPL, and it must be negative (less than zero) in the case of BMI. If the condition is not satisfied, no branch is performed and execution continues with the instruction immediately following the branch instruction.

Example 2.6   Write a section of code that will decrement the content of location 10 by one if it currently contains a negative value, increment it by one if it contains a positive value, and leave it unchanged otherwise:

```
(0)  LOAD   10   **IF CONTENT OF LOC 10  NEGATIVE -
(1)  BMI    5     *THEN CONTINUE AT LOC 5
(2)  BZE    8     *ELSE IF IT IS ZERO - DONE
(3)  LDI    1    **CONT. IS POSITIVE, LOAD 1 AND
(4)  BR     6     *GO TO ADDITION
(5)  LDI   -1    **CONT. IS NEGATIVE, LOAD -1
(6)  ADD         **ADD 1 OR -1 TO VAL. FROM LOC 10
(7)  STORE 10    *AND UPDATE CONT OF LOC. 10
(8)  .....
```

The program performs as follows: first the content of location 10 is loaded on the stack (instr. 0) to be tested for a negative value (instr. 1) and then for a zero (instr. 2). If the content is positive, a 1 is added to the previously loaded value; if the content is negative, a − 1 is added. Otherwise, no action is taken; the program continues with the next instruction in location 8.

Note: Any MICOS program is loaded into memory for execution starting at location 0. In the above program the leading numbers 0 through 8 indicate the location in which the corresponding instruction will reside when the program is loaded. (These numbers are not supplied by the programmer.)

In the above example, each instruction is followed by a verbal description of its function. Such statements are referred to as *comments* and are discussed in the following section.

2.4 USE OF COMMENTS

To increase the readability of programs it is essential to provide extensive documentation. Comments are an important part of this documentation and are inserted directly into the code. Some conventions must be used to designate a sequence of characters as a comment in order to separate it from the code. In the MICOS assembly language there are two ways to designate a sequence of characters to be a comment:

1. An asterisk in the first column of a line designates the entire line as a comment line.
2. Any sequence of characters separated by more than 5 blanks from the last character of an instruction is considered a comment.

In the second case, the comment does not have to begin with an asterisk, however, throughout this book we will use the asterisk with any comment to visually separate it from the program.

A comment is intended only to improve the readability of a program and will be ignored by the machine during translation and execution of the program.

In order for a comment to be useful, it should extend over a sequence of several lines rather than describe the effect of each individual instruction separately. Throughout this handbook the following conventions are used:

- The first line of a comment will begin with two asterisks.
- Each subsequent line considered part of the same comment will begin with one asterisk indented by one position to the right (see example 2.6).

2.5 SYMBOLIC ADDRESSING

So far only the actual location numbers were used with instructions when referring to a particular location. This is a very tedious and error prone way of specifying desired locations, especially with large programs that require frequent alteration during their development; for each instruction deleted from or inserted into the program the locations of all subsequent instructions and data constants change and hence all operands referring to those locations have to be updated to reflect the new numbers.

To alleviate this burden, the programmer can assign names to locations as symbolic addresses, and refer to these instead of the actual location numbers. Since the symbolic names remain with their corresponding instructions or data constants regardless of their current locations, no changes in operands are necessary due to insertions or deletions in the program. The actual location numbers are substituted for the symbolic addresses by the assembler.

A symbolic address, referred to as *label*, is an arbitrary sequence of one to six alphanumeric characters where the first character must be alphabetic, i.e., a letter. Examples of legal labels are ABCDEF, LABELS, S95, XGY8, A8B7C.

A label may be placed in front of any instruction and it must begin in the *first column* of the respective line. By using that label as an operand the same effect is achieved as if the actual location number were used. For example, the instruction BR ABC will cause execution to continue with the instruction labeled ABC.

Example 2.7   The following program has been derived from example 2.6 by replacing the location numbers of branch instructions with symbolic addresses. (We have assumed that the value to be tested resides in the location labeled TSTVAL.)

```
              LOAD   TSTVAL
              BMI    VALNEG
              BZE    DONE
              LDI    1
              BR     ADD
       VALNEG LDI    -1
       ADD    ADD
              STORE  TSTVAL
       DONE   ...
```

To enhance the symbolic addressing capability, the assembler allows a label to be modified by adding to it or subtracting from it an integer value. The operand field may have one of the following forms,

$$LAB + n \quad or$$
$$LAB - n$$

where LAB may be any label within the program and n is an integer. The operand $LAB + n$ then refers to the memory location obtained by adding the number n to the location number corresponding to the label LAB. Similarly, the value n is subtracted from the location number of LAB in the case of $LAB - n$.

Example 2.8

```
           LOAD XYZ
           BZE  LL+1
           BR   LL
           ...
       LL  ADD
           SUB
           ...
```

This program segment first loads the content of location XYZ on top of the stack. If that value is zero, the next instruction BZE will branch to the instruction SUB residing in the location LL + 1. Otherwise, execution continues with the instruction BR   LL which branches to the label LL where execution continues with the instructions ADD, SUB, etc.

2.6 PSEUDO-INSTRUCTIONS

Any program written in the MICOS assembly language must be translated into a corresponding program in the machine language that can be executed by the interpreter.

Two types of assembly language instructions can be distinguished with respect to their translation: *executable* instructions and *pseudo* instructions. Executable instructions are directly converted into their machine language equivalents by the *assembler*. All instructions introduced so far were executable instructions. Pseudo instructions, on the other hand, are not translated into machine language instructions executed as part of the program; rather they are used to instruct the assembler to perform certain tasks while translating a program. *No* machine language instructions are produced for pseudo instructions.

In the MICOS system, two pseudo instructions, DATA and BLOCK, exist. Their purpose is to define the data area of a program which is used by the executable instructions.

```
┌─────────────────┐
│                 │
│                 │
│   DATA c        │
│                 │
│                 │
└─────────────────┘
```

This pseudo instruction causes the assembler to reserve a word of memory, and to preset its contents to the value of the decimal constant c supplied as part of the instruction. For each DATA instruction a separate word of memory is generated.

Note that *no* machine language opcode is produced as is the case with executable instructions; the entire word is used to hold the data constant.

This constant must be an integer between -8388608 and $+8388607$; any value outside of this range will cause an error. The legal range is imposed by the size of the memory word (24 bits), as will be discussed in chapter 3.

The most common usage of the DATA pseudo instruction is to define a constant to be used by some executable instruction of the program. Consider the example of section 2.1 which illustrates the use of the instruction LOAD. There it was assumed that the location 5 contained the value 256. The DATA instruction may be used to generate such a constant.

Symbolic addressing may be employed in the same way as with executable instructions: a label is attached to the DATA pseudo instruction. This label is used by executable instructions to refer to the data constant instead of the actual location number.

Example 2.9   The following section of code illustrates the use of DATA.

```
LOAD A  **LOAD CONTENT OF LOC. A ON STACK
   .
   .
   .
A DATA 10·**THIS LOC. CONTAINS THE
         *CONSTANT 10
```

Sometimes the programmer wishes to use hexadecimal numbers in his/her program. (For a discussion of number systems refer to appendix F.) Rather than converting a hexadecimal number to its decimal equivalent, it can be supplied directly with the DATA pseudo instruction by enclosing it in quotes preceded by the character X. The pseudo instruction then has the form DATA X'hexadecimal constant.'

Example 2.10

```
X DATA 255
Y DATA X'FF'
```

With the above statements, both locations X and Y will contain the same value; the hexadecimal constant FF corresponds to the decimal value 255.

```
┌─────────────────┐
│                 │
│     BLOCK n     │
│                 │
└─────────────────┘
```

This pseudo instruction is used to reserve n words of memory to be used by the program as (temporary) storage spaces, e.g., to hold intermediate results. The contents of all reserved words are preset to zero.

Example 2.11

```
        LOAD  A    **LOAD CONTENT OF LOCATION A AND
        STORE B    *STORE IT IN THE TWO MEMORY
        LOAD  B    *LOCATIONS RESERVED BY THE
        STORE B+1  *BLOCK PSEUDO INSTRUCTION
          .
          .
          .
      A DATA  1    **RESERVE ONE WORD PRESET TO 1
      B BLOCK 2    **RESERVE TWO WORDS (PRESET TO 0)
```

Before execution of the above section of code the location labeled A contains the constant 1. This is followed by two words starting at location B, both of which are preset to zero. After execution of the two STORE instructions, both of these locations (B and B + 1) contain the constant 1 as is illustrated in figure 2.6.

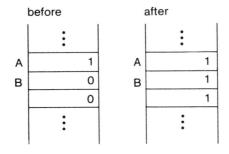

Figure 2.6

2.7 LOGICAL INSTRUCTIONS

In order to understand the function of logical operations, it is necessary to realize that all values (data and instructions) are stored in memory locations in their binary form. For example, the pseudo instruction DATA 11 will reserve a word of memory and preset it to the (decimal) value 11. This value is stored in its binary form, thus the actual contents of the 24-bit word is 0000 0000 0000 0000 0000 1011. (In the following, binary numbers will be shown in groups of 4 for easier reading; internally the blanks are of course not present.) Note that the same binary value would be created with the pseudo instruction DATA X'B'.

Negative numbers are stored in the MICOS system in the two's complement representation. (See appendix F for a discussion of number systems.)
For example, the pseudo instruction DATA -11 would reserve a word of
memory with the following binary content: 1111 1111 1111 1111 1111 0101.

The MICOS system supports the four most common logical functions
'and', 'or', 'exclusive or', and *'complement',* all of which are defined over
the Boolean values 0 and 1. Each of these functions may be described in the
form of a truth table which specifies the value of the function for each possible combination of operands.

MICOS provides four instructions corresponding to the above four logical
functions. Each of these instructions operates on 24-bit words by applying the
corresponding logical function to all 24 bits in parallel.

```
┌─────────────────┐
│                 │
│      AND        │
│                 │
└─────────────────┘
```

This instruction removes the two top-most values of the stack, combines
these by applying the logical AND function to all individual bit-pairs, and
returns the result to the stack.

The logical AND function yields a one only when both operands 1 *and* 2
are equal to one. The truth table for the logical AND function is as follows:

Operand 1	Operand 2	Result
0	0	0
0	1	0
1	0	0
1	1	1

Example 2.12

```
        LOAD    A
        LDI     15
        AND
        STORE   A
        .

        .

        .
    A DATA   X'EFB'
```

The program performs as follows. First the content of location A is loaded on the stack. This is the hexadecimal constant EFB corresponding to the binary number 0000 0000 0000 1110 1111 1011. Then the value 15, in binary 0000 . . . 0000 1111, is loaded on the stack. The two values are combined by applying the logical AND function to all 24 bit-pairs and the result, in binary 0000 . . . 000 1011, is stored in the location A. This value corresponds to the hexadecimal constant B.

In the above example, the constant value 15 can be viewed as a "mask" which, when ANDed with a hexadecimal number, masks out (extracts) the right-most hexadecimal digit of that number. In the above example the digit B has been extracted; all other digits are set to zero.

Similar to the logical AND operation, this instruction performs the logical OR operation with the two top-most values of the stack, pushing the result on the stack.

The logical function OR yields a one when operand 1 or operand 2 (or both) are equal to one. The truth table for the logical OR function is as follows:

```
Operand 1 | Operand 2 || Result

    0     |     0     ||   0
    0     |     1     ||   1
    1     |     0     ||   1
    1     |     1     ||   1
```

Example 2.13   A logical OR operation with the hexadecimal constants FCD and 12A results in the constant FEF, as can be seen when the binary representations, 0000 0000 0000 1111 1100 1101 and 0000 0000 0000 0001 0010 1010, of the above hexadecimal numbers are considered.

```
┌─────────────────────────────────┐
│                                 │
│        EOR (exclusive or)       │
│                                 │
└─────────────────────────────────┘
```

Similar to the logical AND and logical OR operations, this instruction performs the Exclusive OR operation on the two top-most values of the stack.

The logical function EOR yields a one when either operand 1 *or* operand 2 is one, but *not both*. The truth table for the Exclusive OR function is as follows:

Operand 1	Operand 2	Result
0	0	0
0	1	1
1	0	1
1	1	0

Example 2.14 Exclusive OR operation with the hexadecimal constant FCD (in binary 0000 0000 0000 1111 1100 1101) and 12A (in binary 0000 0000 0000 0001 0010 1010) results in the constant EE7 (in binary 0000 0000 0000 1110 1110 0111).

The EOR instruction is frequently used to complement (change from zero to one and vice versa) certain bits of a word. For this purpose a "mask" is created which contains one's in the positions to be complemented. When the mask is Exclusively ORed with another word the desired bits of that word are complemented.

Example 2.15 The following segment of code complements the 6 right-most bits of the word labeled A.

```
        LOAD  A
        LOAD  MSK·
        EOR
        STORE A
        .
        .
        .
MSK DATA  X'3F'
A    ...
```

Assume, for example, that the contents of location A is 5 (in binary 0000 ... 0000 0101). The mask MSK, which is the hexadecimal number 3F (in binary 0000 ... 0000 0011 1111), will complement the 6 right-most bits of the constant 5 yielding the hexadecimal number 3A (in binary 0000 ... 0000 0011 1010).

```
┌─────────────┐
│             │
│             │
│    COMP     │
│             │
│             │
└─────────────┘
```

This instruction performs the logical complement function on the top-of-stack value.

The complement function yields the value zero when the operand is one and vice versa. The truth table for the logical complement is as follows:

Operand	‖	Result
0	‖	1
1	‖	0

Example 2.16   The COMP instruction applied to the hexadecimal constant FFA2 yields the constant FF005D. To understand this result it is necessary to consider the binary representation of the operand which is the 24-bit number 0000 0000 1111 1111 1010 0010. When the logical complement operation is performed, all 24 bits are reversed, resulting in the binary number 1111 1111 0000 0000 0101 1101, corresponding to the constant FF005D.

It is important to note that the logical complement is equivalent to the one's complement operation (see appendix F). Thus, the above constant FF005D actually represents a negative number (the left-most bit is one). Since MICOS uses the two's complement representation for negative numbers, the constant FF005D corresponds to the negative number − FFA3 (one's complement plus one).

2.8 SHIFT INSTRUCTIONS

SHL (*sh*ift *l*eft)

This instruction performs a left-shift operation by 1 bit on the top-of-stack value. The left-most bit is thereby lost since it is shifted "outside" of the 24-bit word. The right-most bit is padded with a zero.

Note that the left-shift operation is equivalent to a multiplication by 2. Executing the left-shift operation n times is then equivalent to a multiplication by 2^n.

Example 2.17

```
LOAD   X
SHL
SHL
STORE X
   .
   .
   .
X DATA  3
```

The content of location X, (in binary 11) is loaded on the stack, left-shifted twice (resulting in 1100), and stored back in location X. Thus the location X contains a value corresponding to (decimal) 12, which is the result of the multiplication $3*2^2 = 3*4$.

When performing the left-shift operation it is important to keep in mind that the operand is kept in a 24-bit word. Since the left-most bit determines the sign of a number, a left-shift operation can change a positive number to a negative one and vice versa. Consider, for example, the hexadecimal number 400001 (in binary 0100 0000 0000 0000 0000 0001). When left-shifted, a one is moved to the left-most bit; thus the word contains the binary number 1000 0000 0000 0000 0000 0010 (in hexadecimal 800002), which corresponds to the negative hexadecimal number $-7FFFFE$.

When this number is left-shifted one more position, the left-most bit is lost, resulting in the binary number 0000 . . . 0000 0100, which corresponds to the positive value 4.

SHR (*sh*ift *r*ight)

Similar to SHL, this instruction performs a right-shift operation by 1 bit on the top-of-stack value. The right-most bit is lost and the left-most bit is padded with a zero or a one depending on the current left-most bit (the sign bit) of the value being shifted. This is necessary in order to guarantee that negative numbers remain negative when right-shifted. Note that a right-shift operation corresponds to an integer division by 2.

Example 2.18

$$\text{LDI} \quad -12$$
$$\text{SHR}$$

After execution of the above two instructions, the top-of-stack will have the value − 6. This corresponds to the binary (two's complement) representation 1111 1111 1111 1111 1111 1010, obtained by right-shifting the binary (two's complement) representation of − 12, 1111 1111 1111 1111 1111 0100.

2.9 INPUT/OUTPUT INSTRUCTIONS

In order to allow the program to communicate with the user, two files named DATA and RES are provided, which hold the program's input and output data respectively. The program may obtain data values from the file DATA and it may output results into the file RES. This is accomplished using the following input/output instructions.

```
┌─────────────────────────────────┐
│                                 │
│            INPUT M              │
│                                 │
└─────────────────────────────────┘
```

This instruction causes one integer to be transferred from the DATA file to the memory location M.

The DATA file may contain only decimal integers, each of which must be in the range between −8388608 and +8388607. Individual values must be separated from one another by one or more blanks.

It is the responsibility of the programmer to ensure that the DATA file contains as many (or more) integers as will be requested by the program during execution, otherwise an error will occur.

Example 2.19 Assume that the input file contains the sequence of integers 1, 2 ... 9. The following program then transfers the values 1, 2, and 3 into the locations DAT, DAT + 3, and DAT + 2, respectively. Note that the location DAT + 1 remains unchanged. This is illustrated in figure 2.7.

```
                    INPUT DAT
                    INPUT DAT+3
                    INPUT DAT+2
                       .
                       .
                       .
          DAT BLOCK 4
```

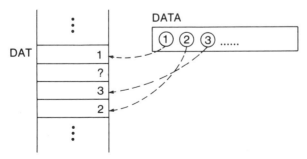

Figure 2.7

It should be noted that the INPUT instruction overwrites any previous contents (data or instructions) of the memory locations into which data is to be transferred from the input file. For example, the following (not necessarily useful) program will overwrite the instruction BR and the previously defined data constant 5 with the next two values read from the input file.

```
        INPUT X
        INPUT X+1
            .
            .
            .
      X BR     Y
        DATA   5
```

```
┌─────────────────┐
│                 │
│    OUTPUT M     │
│                 │
└─────────────────┘
```

This instruction causes one integer value to be transferred from the memory location M to the output file RES. All output values are decimal integers, each of which is placed on a new line in the RES file.

Example 2.20 Write a section of code that will input two values from the input file and compute their sum. If that sum is positive it should be output, otherwise a zero is to be output.

```
        INPUT  A     **INPUT 2 VALUES
        INPUT  A+1   *
        LOAD   A     **ADD THESE VALUES
        LOAD   A+1   *
        ADD          *
        BMI    OUT   **IF SUM IS NEGATIVE GO TO OUTPUT
        STORE  RSLT  *ELSE OVERWRITE RSLT WITH SUM
 OUT    OUTPUT RSLT **OUTPUT RESULT (ZERO OR SUM)
          .
          .
          .
 A      BLOCK  2     **2 WORDS TO HOLD INPUT
 RSLT   DATA   0     **RESULT TO BE OUTPUT.
```

After execution of the above program, the output file RES will contain the result of the computation; this is the sum of the values in the locations A and A + 1 if that sum is positive, otherwise, it is the value zero.

2.10 ADDRESSING MODES

Instructions can be classified according to the number and location of their operands. With the instructions discussed so far three modes of addressing were implicitly introduced: immediate, direct, and stack addressing.

Immediate addressing is the simplest way to specify an operand. Here the instruction contains the operand itself rather than a location or other information describing where the operand is to be fetched from. An example of immediate addressing is the instruction LDI c where the operand (constant) c is supplied as part of the instruction.

In the case of *direct* addressing the operand is stored in a memory location distinct from that where the instruction is kept. The address of that location is then supplied as part of the instruction.

The instructions INPUT M and OUTPUT M, as well as all of the branch instructions presented in previous sections, make use of direct addressing. For example, in the case of the LOAD M instruction, the operand loaded on the stack is the content of the memory location M.*

Stack addressing refers to an addressing mode where the operands are found on the stack. Examples of instructions using stack addressing are COMP, SHL, SHR (using the current top-of-stack value as the operand), and all other logical and arithmetic instructions (using the two top-most values of the stack as their operands).

In the following sections, two other important addressing modes—*indirect* and *indexed*—provided in the MICOS system shall be presented.

Indirect addressing

As discussed above, direct addressing is a scheme where the instruction contains the address of the operand. Indirect addressing, on the other hand, is a scheme in which the address within the instruction specifies a location which holds not the operand itself, but the address of the operand. In other words, the instruction contains the address of the address of the operand.

Indirect addressing is indicated within the instruction by ataching the character I to the address field of the instruction, separated by a comma.

---

*Depending on the point of view, the instructions LOAD and STORE could also be considered as using both direct and stack addressing since the value to be loaded/stored is moved between a memory location and the stack.

Example 2.21   Compare the following two load instructions:

```
LOAD M
LOAD M,I
  .
  .
  .
M DATA 100
```

The first instruction uses direct addressing, thus the content of the location M (the value 100) will be loaded on the stack (see figure 2.8a).

The second instruction uses indirect addressing, hence the content of the location M is interpreted not as the operand but as its address. Therefore, the content *x* of the location 100 will be loaded on the stack rather than the value 100 itself (figure 2.8b).

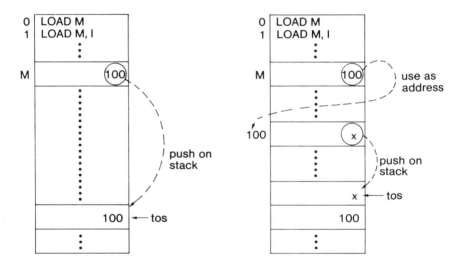

Figure 2.8

Indexed addressing

This addressing scheme utilizes a special-purpose register called the *index register,* which exists as part of the MICOS processor. The content of the index register may be loaded or modified using a set of special instructions introduced in section 2.11. The purpose of indexing is to vary the operand address specified within an instruction by adding to it the content of the index register. The programmer may specify indexing using the character X attached to the address field of the instruction, separated by a comma.

The size of the index register is 24 bits, which implies that the smallest and the largest integer the index register can hold are -8388608 and $+8388607$, respectively.

Example 2.22   Compare the following two load instructions:

```
            LOAD M
            LOAD M,X
                .
                .
                .
          M DATA 100
            DATA 200
```

The first instruction, using direct addressing, will cause the content of location M (the value 100) to be loaded on the stack (figure 2.9a).

The second instruction uses indexing, which implies that the operand is fetched from the location obtained by adding the current content of the index register to the location M. In the above example, if the content of the index register were zero, then the value 100 (the content of location $M + 0$) would be loaded; if the content of the index register were one, then the value 200 (the content of location $M + 1$) would be loaded (figure 2.9b).

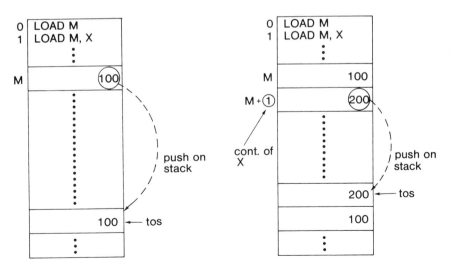

Figure 2.9

Both indexing and indirection may be used together with the same instruction. In this case the content of the index register is added to the address specified in the instruction. This modified address is then used to fetch a word of memory which is interpreted as the address of the operand.

Example 2.23   Consider the following section of code:

```
LOAD M,I,X
        .
        .
        .
M DATA 100
  DATA 200
```

Assuming that the content of the index register is 1, the content of the location M + 1 (the data constant 200) will be fetched and interpreted as the address of the operand. Hence, the actual operand will be the content of location 200 (not shown in the program).

2.11 INDEX REGISTER MANIPULATION

The following instructions are used to load, store, or update the content of the index register.

```
┌─────────────────────────────────────┐
│                                       │
│     LDX M (load index register)       │
│                                       │
└─────────────────────────────────────┘
```

Analogous to the instruction LOAD, the instruction LDX causes the content of the memory location M to be loaded into the index register. The content of the location M itself remains unchanged, as was the case with the instruction LOAD.

```
┌─────────────────────────────────────┐
│                                       │
│     LDXI c (load index immediate)     │
│                                       │
└─────────────────────────────────────┘
```

This instruction is the immediate-addressing version of loading the index register. Here the constant value c specified within the instruction is loaded into the index register. This is analogous to the instruction LDI which loads a constant value on the stack. As was the case with the instruction LDI, the constant c must be an integer in the range between -2048 and 2047; otherwise an error will occur.

```
TSX (transfer stack to index register)
```

This instruction causes the top-of-stack value to be copied into the index register. The top-of-stack value is thereby removed from the stack, as was the case with the instruction STORE.

```
TXS (transfer index register to stack)
```

This instruction has the reverse effect of the instruction TSX. It causes the content of the index register to be pushed on top of the stack. The content of the index register remains unchanged, only a copy is moved to the stack.

```
INX (increment index register)
```

This instruction increments the current content of the index register by one. As with the instruction ADD, an attempt to increment the index register above the maximum value, $+8388607$, will result in an error.

```
┌─────────────────────────────────────────┐
│                                           │
│        DEX (decrement index register)     │
│                                           │
└─────────────────────────────────────────┘
```

Similar to INX, this instruction decrements the current content of the index register by one. As with the instruction SUB, an attempt to decrement the index register below the value -8388608 will result in an error.

The main purpose of indexed addressing is to allow the same section of code to operate on different values stored in consecutive memory locations. The following example illustrates this idea.

Example 2.24 Write a program which reads 100 values from the input file DATA into 100 consecutive locations starting at the label A.

The following is one possible (but rather "inelegant") solution to this problem.

```
         LDXI   -100    **PRESET X TO 100 ITERATIONS
NEXTNR   IVEC   A+100,X **INPUT INTO A+100+CONT(X)
         INX            **INCR. X AND MOVE IT TO STACK
         TXS             *TO TEST IT FOR ZERO
         BZE    DONE    **IF ZERO IS REACHED - DONE
         TSX             *ELSE REMOVE VALUE FROM STACK
         BR     NEXTNR   *AND BRANCH TO INPUT NEXT NO.
DONE     ...
         ...
A        BLOCK  100     **100 WORDS TO HOLD INPUT
```

A rather awkward feature may be observed in the above program: in order to test the content of the index register (to terminate the execution), it is necessary to move it to the stack (TXS) since no instruction which would allow the index register to be tested directly has yet been presented. After the test is completed, the tested value is removed from the stack to prevent a growth of the stack at each iteration. In the above example the instruction TSX is used to move that value back to the index register. (The removal could be accomplished also with the instruction POP presented in section 2.15.)

A more elegant solution to the above problem would be possible if the content of the index register could be tested directly without having to move it to the stack. Three instructions which permit such a test are presented in the following section.

2.12 LOOPS

Many problems require performing the same operation on a sequence of values stored in consecutive memory locations. For such problems a scheme, referred to as a *loop*, is necessary. This allows a section of code to be repeated for each element of the sequence of values. An example of such a loop has been presented in section 2.11. When analyzing the body of this loop (the code repeated), it can be seen that only the instruction IVEC actually operates on the sequence of data to be transferred. All other instructions perform only administrative tasks of testing and maintaining the content of the index register. Since such tasks repeat in a similar form for most types of loops, the following three instructions have been provided which allow a conditional branch to be performed depending on the current content of the index register.

BXZE M (*b*ranch on inde*x* *ze*ro)
BXPL M (*b*ranch on inde*x* *pl*us or zero)
BXMI M (*b*ranch on inde*x* *mi*nus)

These instructions are analogous to the instructions BZE, BPL, and BMI presented in section 2.3. A conditional branch to the location M is performed if the current condition of the index register satisfies the respective condition, i.e., it must be zero in the case of BXZE, it must be non-negative (greater than or equal to zero) in the case of BXPL, and it must be negative (less than zero) in the case of BXMI. Otherwise, no branch is performed and execution continues with the instruction immediately following the branch instruction.

Example 2.25   Consider again the problem of section 2.11. The use of the BXMI instruction eliminates the need to transfer the content of the index register to the stack to test it for zero. The "administrative tasks" of the loop have been reduced to the two instructions INX and BXMI.

```
        LDXI   -100     **PRESET X TO 100 ITERATIONS
NEXTNR  INPUT  A+100,X  **INPUT VALUE INTO A+100+CONT(X)
        INX             *AND INCREMENT X
        BXMI   NEXTNR   **REPEAT FOR NEXT VALUE
          .
          .
          .
A       BLOCK 100       **100 WORDS TO HOLD ARRAY
```

2.13 SUBROUTINES

Most programs contain segments of code performing the same task in different parts of the program. The idea of a subroutine is to eliminate repetitive codes by providing only *one* copy of the desired code and to allow the program to "reuse" it whenever necessary. Such a segment of code is referred to as a *subroutine* and it may be executed (called) using a special instruction BRSUB which branches to the specified subroutine.

When the subroutine has completed its task, it must return to the calling program. The instruction RET is used by the subroutine for this purpose. After returning to the calling program, execution continues with the instruction immediately following the calling instruction BRSUB. The address of this instruction is referred to as the *return address*. Since the subroutine may be invoked anywhere within the program, the return address must be transmitted to the subroutine so that it knows where to return to. In MICOS the return address is placed on the stack at the time the subroutine is called.

BRSUB M (*br*anch to *sub*routine)

This instruction causes a branch to the instruction labeled M. This transfer of control is very similar to the effect of the instruction BR M, however, in addition to performing the branch, the instruction BRSUB places the return address (the address of the instruction following BRSUB) on top of the stack. This address is branched to by the subroutine after completion of its task. This is accomplished via the instruction RET.

RET (*ret*urn)

This instruction designates the end of a subroutine. It causes a branch to the address currently on top of the stack, allowing the subroutine to return to the calling program. The return address is removed from the stack by the RET instruction.

Note: The instruction RET interprets any value currently on top of the stack as the return address. Thus, it is the responsibility of the programmer to ensure that the correct address is on top of the stack when the instruction RET is encountered. This implies that values placed on the stack by the subroutine (e.g., any intermediate results) must be removed to expose the return address before RET is executed.

Example 2.26 Write a subroutine NSQR which calculates the square of the value in location N and overwrites that value with the result. (Hint: A square value may be calculated by repeated addition.)

This subroutine is to be called from a program, MAIN, which reads values from the input file, calls the subroutine NSQR, and outputs the squares of the input values as calculated by NSQR.

```
*BEGIN OF MAIN PROGRAM
MAIN    INPUT   N      **INPUT VALUE TO BE SQUARED
        BRSUB   NSQR   **CALCULATE N SQUARE AND
        OUTPUT  N       *OUTPUT RESULT
        BR      MAIN   **REPEAT MAIN PROGR. FOREVER
N       BLOCK   1      **INPUT/OUTPUT VALUE
*BEGIN OF SUBROUTINE
NSQR    LDX     N      **PRESET X TO N ITERATIONS
        DEX             *
        LDI     0      **LOAD INITIAL RESULT
NXTADD  DEX            **DECREMENT X
        LOAD    N      **ADD N TO PREVIOUSLY COMPUTED
        ADD             *PARTIAL SUM
        BXPL    NXTADD **REPEAT THE ABOVE N TIMES
        STORE   N      **STORE RESULT INTO N
        RET            **DONE - RETURN TO MAIN
```

A subroutine may be placed anywhere within the main program. However, it must be guaranteed that it will be reached only via a BRSUB instruction. This will be the case only if the instruction immediately preceding the subroutine is BR, RET, HALT (to be presented in section 2.15), or one of the pseudo instructions. In all other cases the subroutine would be entered directly as part of the main program and not as a subroutine. (Note that the beginning of a subroutine is no different from any other instruction with a label.)

In this case no return address would be pushed on the stack and the RET instruction would cause an error by interpreting the current top-of-stack value as the expected return address.

2.14 PARAMETER PASSING

When employing a subroutine, it is necessary to pass data values from the main program to the subroutine and, similarly, to pass results back to the main program. In MICOS there are two places where these values, called *parameters,* may be kept while transferring control to and from the subroutine. These are any of the memory locations defined with DATA or BLOCK pseudo instructions, or the stack.

In the example of section 2.13, the first method was implicitly introduced; the value to be squared was kept in a memory location N. The following example shows the skeleton of a subroutine which performs the same task of squaring a value; this time, however, the value to be squared is placed on the stack before calling the subroutine. Similarly, the result is returned to the main program by placing it on the stack.

```
*BEGIN OF CALLING PROGRAM
MAIN    INPUT  N      **INPUT VALUE TO BE SQUARED
        LOAD   N       *AND PLACE IT ON STACK
        BRSUB  NSQR    **CALCULATE N SQUARE
        STORE  N        *STORE IT IN N AND
        OUTPUT N        *OUTPUT IT
        BR     MAIN    **REPEAT MAIN PROG. FOREVER
*BEGIN OF SUBROUTINE
XSQR    STORE  RETADR **SAVE RETURN ADDRESS
          .
          .           **REPLACE TOS WITH ITS SQUARE
          .
        LOAD   RETADR **RESTORE RETURN ADDRESS
        RET            **DONE - RETURN TO MAIN
RETADR  BLOCK  1       **TEMP. STORAGE FOR RETURN ADDR.
```

Since the return address is also transmitted to the subroutine on the stack, the subroutine must first save this address in a temporary location (RETADR) in order to expose the value to be squared. Before reaching the RET instruction the return address must be returned to the stack.

2.15 OTHER INSTRUCTIONS

```
┌─────────────────┐
│                 │
│      POP        │
│                 │
└─────────────────┘
```

This instruction causes the current top-of-stack value to be "popped" (removed) from the stack and discarded. It may be used to remove intermediate results, e.g., values loaded on the stack for the purpose of being tested (with a conditional branch instruction), or to expose the return address in a subroutine before executing the RET instruction.

```
┌─────────────────┐
│                 │
│      HALT       │
│                 │
└─────────────────┘
```

This instruction causes the execution of a program to terminate. The HALT instruction must be the last instruction to be executed in any MICOS program.

The most common (and recommended) organization of a MICOS program is as follows:

```
— — —
— — —          executable instruction of main program
— — —
— — —
HALT
— — —
— — —          global data area, i.e., data constants
— — —          and reserved memory blocks referenced
— — —          in both the main program and the subroutines
— — —
— — —
```

```
— — —
— — —        executable instructions of subroutine i
— — —
— — —
RET
— — —        local data area, i.e., data constants and
— — —        reserved memory blocks referenced only
— — —        by subroutine i
   .
   .
   .
```

Chapter 3

TRANSLATION OF ASSEMBLY PROGRAMS

All user programs are written in a symbolic language, the assembly language, which facilitates the programming task. For execution, each program must be translated into its machine language equivalent. This task is performed by a program called the *assembler* which converts a) each executable instruction into the corresponding machine language instruction, and b) each pseudo instruction into one or more data constants.

For each submitted program the assembler produces two files, OBJ and LIST. OBJ is called the *object file*; it contains the translated program which is read and executed by the interpreter (see also section 7.1). LIST is called the *listing file*; it shows the program as submitted to the assembler and its translation into machine language. (The format of the listing file is summarized in appendix D.)

Note: The OBJ file contains an internally encoded form of the translated program intended only to be used by the interpreter. To examine the machine program in its proper hexadecimal form, the file LIST should be considered by the programmer.

3.1 TRANSLATION OF EXECUTABLE INSTRUCTIONS

For each executable instruction of an assembly program, the assembler generates exactly one machine instruction which is a sequence of 24 bits organized as follows:

23	22	21	20	19 – 12	11 – 0
–	–	i	x	opcode	operand

$$i = \text{indirect bit}$$
$$x = \text{index bit}$$

37

Bits 23 and 22 are *unused* and will be set to zero by the assembler.

Bit 21 is the *indirection bit*. It is set to one by the assembler if the instruction being translated contains the character "I", indicating indirect addressing (see section 2.10). If indirect addressing is not specified, this bit is set to zero.

Bit 20 is the *index bit*. Similar to the indirection bit, it is set to one by the assembler if the instruction being translated contains the character "X", indicating indexed addressing. Otherwise, it is set to zero.

Bits 19–12 contain the *opcode*. The assembler places into these bits the numeric (binary) value corresponding to the symbolic opcode of the instruction being translated. The numeric values for all opcodes may be found in appendix A. (There, the values are given in hexadecimal for easier reading.) For example, the opcode LOAD is translated to 00000000 in bits 19–12, the opcode LDI is translated 00000001, etc. . . . .

Bits 11–0 contain the *operand*. The following cases can occur:

• Memory addressing is used. Here the instruction contains the (direct or indirect) address of the operand (as for example in LOAD A). In this case the assembler places into bits 11–0 the (binary) number corresponding to the specified memory address.

• Immediate addressing is used. Here the instruction contains the operand itself, as for example in LDI 1. In this case the bits 11–0 contain the specified constant. (Two's complement representation is used for negative numbers.)

• Stack addressing is used. The instruction contains no operand at all, as, for example, in ADD. In this case the bits 11–0 are set to zero and will be ignored by the interpreter.

In all of the above cases the size of the operand field (12 bits) imposes a restriction on the size of the operand: the largest integer that can be represented in 12 bits is $+2047$, and similarly, the smallest integer that can be represented in 12 bits (using the two's complement representation) is -2048. (See appendix D for a discussion of number systems.)

Example 3.1   The following lines of code present a sequence of instructions in three different forms:

1. The first block shows the binary form of the machine instruction. This is the form in which the instruction is actually stored in memory for execution.
2. The second block shows the same machine instruction in the hexadecimal representation. This is the form produced by the assembler as part of the listing.
3. The third block shows the symbolic form of the instruction. This is the form in which it has been written by the programmer.

Remark: In the last two instructions, it has been assumed that the label A corresponds to the memory address 9.

```
0000 0000 0001 0000 0000 1100    00100C    LDI    12
0000 0000 1100 1111 1111 0100    00CFF4    LDXI  -12
0000 0010 1110 0000 0000 0000    02E000    HALT
0010 0000 0000 0000 0000 1001    200009    LOAD  A,I
0011 0000 0010 0000 0000 1001    302009    STORE A,I,X
```

3.2 TRANSLATION OF PSEUDO INSTRUCTIONS

The pseudo instruction DATA reserves one word of memory preset to the specified constant. Within the pseudo instruction this constant may be given in decimal or hexadecimal (see section 2.6); the machine language equivalent will always be stored in its binary form. On the listing, however, this binary number is shown in the hexadecimal representation as was the case with all executable instructions discussed previously. The two's complement representation is used for all negative numbers.

The size of a memory word (24 bits) imposes a restriction on the size of possible data constants. The largest integer that can be represented in 24 bits is 8388607, and similarly, the smallest integer that can be represented in 24 bits (using the two's complement representation) is − 8388608.

Example 3.2 In the following lines of code, column one shows the machine language equivalents of the psuedo instructions shown in column two.

```
000003    DATA 3
00001A    DATA 26
123456    DATA X'123456'
FFFFF4    DATA -12
```

The pseudo instruction BLOCK *n* reserves *n* words of memory all of which are preset to zero (see section 2.6). On the listing produced by the assembler only the first word of any BLOCK is shown.

3.3 DATA VERSUS INSTRUCTIONS

In sections 3.1 and 3.2 we have explained how assembly instructions and data constants are translated by the assembler to form an executable machine program. Both instructions and data constants are translated into strings of 24 bits. Since a data constant may have any value, it is possible to define a constant which, after translation, has exactly the same form as an instruction. Consider, for example, the pseudo instruction DATA X'1009', which defines a hexadecimal constant stored in memory as the following 24-bit string: 0000 0000 0001 0000 0000 1001. Exactly the same 24-bit string will be produced for the instruction LDI 9. Hence the bit string defined with the above DATA pseudo instruction may be executed and will produce the same effect as the instruction LDI 9. In other words, there is no essential difference between the instructions LDI 9 and DATA X'1009' in an assembly program—after the program has been translated it cannot be determined which of the above instructions has been used.

Thus, the distinction between an instruction and a data constant is only a matter of interpretation: *if a memory word is fetched by the interpreter it is treated as an instruction.* For example, a branch to a data constant will result in an attempt by the interpreter to execute that constant. Depending on the value of the constant, this attempt may or may not be successful. *If, on the other hand, a memory word is referenced by an instruction it is treated as a data constant.* For example, using the instruction LOAD, it is possible to load an instruction on top of the stack and to treat it as a data constant.

Example 3.3   The following sections of code are equivalent in that the same machine programs will be produced by the assembler and, hence, the same effect will be achieved when the code is executed.

```
(0)                 LOAD   A      DATA X'5'
(1)                 LDI    1      DATA X'1001'
(2)                 SUB           DATA X'21000'
(3)                 STORE  A      DATA X'2005'
(4)                 HALT          DATA X'2E000'
(5)           A     DATA   X'20'  DATA X'20'
```

Remark: This example is intended only to demonstrate the equality of data and instructions. It does not suggest writing programs using data constants.

The above example shows that constants defined with the DATA pseudo instruction may be interpreted as executable instructions. Similarly, executable instructions may be interpreted as data, being loaded, stored, modified, etc. This technique, called self-modification of programs, was popular in the 'early' days of programming when indexed addressing and other advanced programming techniques were unknown. By allowing a program to modify the operand field of an instruction on each iteration of a loop, it was possible to access different values during each execution of that loop. Since self-modifying programs are very difficult to understand and to debug, this programming technique is strongly discouraged. However, for the sake of completeness we include the following example showing a self-modifying section of code which "moves" the contents of the array A to the array B.

```
BEGIN LOAD    A        **MOVE ONE WORD OF ARRAY A
      STORE   B        **TO ARRAY B
      LOAD    BEGIN    **MODIFY INSTR. AT LABEL 'BEGIN'
      LDI     1        *BY ADDING 1 TO ITS ADDR. FIELD
      ADD              *
      STORE   BEGIN    *
      LOAD    BEGIN+1  **DO THE SAME WITH INSTR. AT
      LDI     1        *LABEL 'BEGIN+1'
      ADD              *
      STORE   BEGIN+1  *
      ...
      BR      BEGIN    **REPEAT MOVE FOR NEXT ARRAY WORD
      ...
A     BLOCK   100      **ARRAY DEFINITIONS
B     BLOCK   100      *
```

During the first execution of the loop the content of the first element of the array A is moved to the first element of the array B. Thereafter the address parts of the LOAD and STORE instructions are incremented to refer to the next word of the respective array. Thus, during the second execution of the loop, the content of A + 1 is moved to B + 1, and so forth. (The termination condition for the loop is not shown in the program.)

PART II

The Microprogramming Level

Chapter 4

PRINCIPLES OF MICROPROGRAMMING

In part I of this handbook we have presented an assembly level language and its executable machine language counterpart. This we have done under the assumption that there exists a processor capable of interpreting the machine language. In the second part of this handbook we are concerned with the implementation of such a processor referred to as the *MICOS interpreter*. This interpreter is not implemented in hardware but is itself a program written in a *microprogramming* language and stored in a separate storage called the *micromemory*. The function of this program is to fetch machine language instructions from the main memory, examine their opcodes and operands (including the indexing and indirection bits), and actually carry out the function specified by each instruction.

The conceptual, simplified organization of the interpreter is as follows:

- Fetch next machine language instruction and store it into a special register (the instruction register). Depending on the opcode of the fetched instruction, branch to the section of code which interprets that instruction.

  Fetch cycle: Code to fetch and decode a machine language instruction

- Interpret LOAD instruction. Return to fetch cycle.

- Interpret LDI instruction. Return to fetch cycle.

  .
  .
  .

- Interpret HALT instruction.

  Execution cycles: Segments of code, each of which interprets a distinct machine language instruction

When the interpretation of a program is started, the interpreter fetches and executes the machine instruction in memory location 0. If this instruction is not a branch, the interpreter fetches and interprets the next instruction in location 1, etc. Only if a branch instruction is fetched is the sequence of execution altered; in this case (if the branch condition is satisfied) the interpreter fetches the next instruction from the memory location specified in the branch instruction.

To further illustrate this principle consider the following situation: assume that the instruction ADD (its machine language equivalent) has been fetched from main memory. The interpreter then branches to the sequence of microinstructions provided to interpret the instruction ADD. This sequence will move the two top-most values of the stack to some internal registers, add these values, and move the result back to the stack. Thereafter it will branch to the beginning of the microprogram where the next machine instruction will be fetched. This sequence is repeated until the HALT instruction is encountered, which causes the interpreter to cease execution.

The MICOS system allows the user to add new execution cycles to the interpreter, thus implementing new instructions at the assembly/machine language level. These are automatically appended to the existing interpreter as will be discussed in section 7.2

4.1 LOW-LEVEL ARCHITECTURE

In order for the interpreter to be able to fulfill its function of interpreting machine language instructions, a number of components invisible to the assembly language programmer, such as temporary registers and their interconnections, must be provided. The complete MICOS architecture is shown in figure 4.1.* It consists of a *memory* unit, an *arithmetic/logic* unit (ALU), a *shift* unit (SHIFTER), an *input/output* (I/O) interface, a set of *24-bit registers,* and a set of *12-bit registers*. All of these components are interconnected by three communication lines called *buses*.

The purpose of the memory unit is to hold the machine language program and the stack as shown in figure 1.2.

The ALU is capable of performing the operations add, subtract, logical AND, logical OR, and Exclusive OR on the two values supplied via the two input buses IN1 and IN2.

---

*It should be noted that this architecture does not really exist in hardware but is only simulated by a program running on a general-purpose computer. However, for the purpose of micro and assembly language programming as presented in this handbook the programmer may assume its existence as an actual hardware machine.

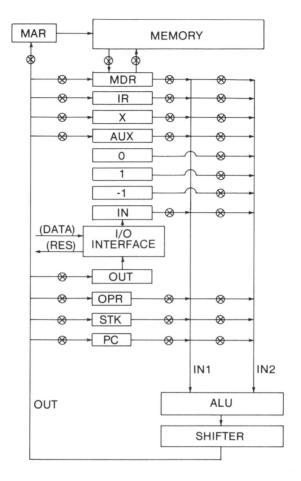

Figure 4.1

The SHIFTER is capable of performing a left-shift or a right-shift operation by one bit on the value produced by the ALU. The result of the shift operation is placed on the output bus OUT.

The I/O interface is provided for communication with the two input/output files DATA and RES.

The two sets of registers fulfill the following functions: The registers MAR and MDR are provided for communication with the memory. In order to read a word from memory, the location number of that word must be placed into MAR—the *m*emory *a*ddress *r*egister and a read operation is specified. The memory retrieves the content of the addressed word and places it into MDR—the *m*emory *d*ata *r*egister. For example, by placing a zero into MAR and issuing a read command, the first instruction of the user program (at address 0) would be read into MDR.

Similarly, to write a word into memory, the desired address is placed into MAR and the write operation is specified. The word to be written into memory is then taken from MDR and placed into the specified location.

The register IR is the *i*nstruction *r*egister; it is used to hold the current machine instruction fetched from memory for execution.

The register X is the inde*x* register introduced in section 2.10. This is the only register visible not only to the programmer at the microprogramming level but also to the assembly language programmer.

The register AUX is an *aux*iliary register; it is used to hold one of the operands during arithmetic or logical operations.

The registers labeled 0, 1, and -1 are *constant* registers; their contents are preset to the values 0, 1, and -1, respectively, and cannot be altered by the microprogram since no connections exist between the output bus and these registers. The constants are used in the interpreter for a variety of arithmetic/logical operations, as will be discussed in chapter 5.

It is important to notice the bit-pattern representing the three constants:

1. The register 0 contains a sequence of 24 zeros.
2. The register -1 contains a sequence of 24 ones (the two's complement representation of -1).
3. The register 1 contains a one in the right-most bit and zeros in the remaining 23 bits.

The registers IN and OUT are connected to the I/O interface which is used to communicate with the input file DATA and the output file RES. The I/O interface transfers values from DATA to IN and similarly from OUT to RES.

The register IN may be visualized as a "window" into the file DATA, showing the next value not yet transferred from DATA. When the value is removed from the register IN, the next value is automatically moved by the I/O interface from DATA to IN.

Similarly, the register OUT provides a "window" into the file RES; when a value is placed into OUT by the interpreter it is automatically transferred to the next free line in RES.

The register OPR is the *oper*and register; it is used to hold the operand of the instruction currently being interpreted.

The register STK is the *stack* pointer; it holds the address of the current top-of-stack (*tos*) value.

The register PC is the *p*rogram *c*ounter; it contains the address of the machine instruction which is to be fetched and executed next. Before execution starts, the PC register is set to zero, causing the first machine instruction to be fetched and executed. During execution this counter is incremented to point to the next instruction or, in the case of a branch instruction, to point to the target instruction specified by the branch instruction.

All of the above components—memory, registers, the ALU, and the SHIFTER—are interconnected via three buses IN1, IN2, and OUT. The existing connections can be seen in figure 4.1. The symbol "⊗" designates a *gate,* which is a hardware component capable of connecting or disconnecting the line on which it is placed. Each microinstruction of the interpreter causes certain gates to open and thus allows data to flow between registers, the ALU/SHIFTER unit, and memory. Hence, the basic function of the microprogram is to open gates in the appropriate sequences to carry out the functions of the machine instructions being interpreted.

To further illustrate this concept, consider the following example: assume that the instruction ADD has been fetched from memory and stored in the instruction register IR. The interpreter will perform the following steps.

- The content of STK (the current *tos* pointer) is transferred to MAR. This is done by gating the content of STK onto the input bus IN1 and the constant 0 onto the other input bus IN2. An add operation is performed in the ALU and the result STK+0 is gated into MAR via the output bus OUT. (No shift operation is performed, the value passes through the SHIFTER unchanged.)
- When the value is stored in MAR, the gate between the memory and the register MDR (the read gate) is opened causing the *tos* value to flow into MDR.
- The value is moved from MDR to AUX by gating it, together with the constant 0, through the ALU/SHIFTER in the same way as STK was transferred to MAR. AUX now contains the former *tos*-value.
- The STK pointer is incremented by one to point to the value next below the *tos*-value (the second operand). This is accomplished by gating STK and the constant 1 through the ALU. The result STK+1 is gated into MAR and the gate between the memory and MDR is opened, allowing the value next below the former *tos*-value to flow into MDR.
- The contents of MDR and AUX, now containing the two top-most values of the stack, are added and the result is gated into MDR. The gate between MDR and the memory (the write gate) is opened allowing the content of MDR to flow back to memory replacing the value currently pointed to by MAR.
- The execution cycle of the machine instruction ADD being interpreted is terminated by a branch to the fetch cycle where the next machine instruction is fetched from memory.

Chapter 5

PROGRAMMING WITH THE MICROPROGRAMMING LANGUAGE

The purpose of this section is to present the symbolic microprogramming language of MICOS and to illustrate the function of individual microinstructions using portions of the actual MICOS interpreter and other examples. The entire listing of the interpreter is included as appendix C.

5.1 MICROINSTRUCTION TYPES

In the microprogramming language two types of instructions—*gate* instructions and *branch* instructions—may be distinguished. The effect of each gate instruction is to open certain gates to allow values to flow between registers, the ALU/SHIFTER unit, and the memory. Branch instructions, on the other hand, do not open any gates but rather cause a (conditional) branch within the microprogram.

Below we will introduce all microprogramming instructions (microinstructions for short, or simply, instructions, when no confusion with machine instructions arises) by developing sections of microcode which interpret certain machine instructions.

5.1.1 Gate Instructions

Each gate instruction consists of an operation code (*opcode* for short) and three to five operands in the following format:

opcode in1,in2,out;shiftop;memop

The opcode specifies the operation performed by the ALU. This can be one of the operations ADD, SUB, AND, OR, or EOR.

The operand "in1" specifies the register to be connected to the input bus IN1 by opening the appropriate gate. (We say the register is gated onto the bus IN1.) It can be any of the registers which has a gate connection to this bus (see figure 4.1).

The operand "in2" specifies the register to be connected to the input bus IN2 by opening the appropriate gate. It can be any of the registers which has a gate connection to this bus.

The operand "out" specifies the register to be connected to the output bus OUT by opening the appropriate gate. It can be any of the registers connected to the output bus.

The above three operands are mandatory and must be specified with any gate instruction, otherwise an error is reported by the microprogram translator. The next two operands "shiftop" and "memop" are optional; each must be separated from any preceding operands by a semicolon.

The operand "shiftop" specifies the operation of the SHIFTER; it may have the value SHL or SHR. In the case of SHL, the output of the ALU is left-shifted by one bit before it is gated into the output register. The left-most bit of the value being shifted is discarded while the right-most bit is padded with a zero.

In the case of SHR, the output of the ALU is right-shifted by one bit before it is gated into the output register. The right-most bit of the value shifted is discarded while the left-most bit is padded with the current sign bit. That is, the left-most bit becomes zero if the number shifted is positive or zero and it becomes one if that number is negative.

If the "shiftop" operand is omitted no shift operation is performed; the result of the ALU simply passes through the SHIFTER unchanged.

The operand "memop" specifies the operation performed by the memory; it can have the value R or W. R specifies a memory read operation. When this operand is present, the current content of the MAR register is interpreted as a memory address and the memory read gate is opened, causing the content of the addressed word to flow into the MDR register. W specifies a memory write operation. When this operand is present, the current content of MAR is interpreted as a memory address and the memory write gate is opened, causing the current content of MDR to be written into the memory location specified by MAR.

For each instruction, the memory read/write operation, if specified, is performed *after* the modification of the output register (operand "out") has been completed. Thus, if an instruction changes the MAR or MDR register, the *new* values are used as the address and data values for the memory read/write operation (see examples in section 5.2).

5.1.2 Branch Instructions

Two types of branch instructions—conditional and unconditional—exist in the microprogramming language. The format of the branch instructions is as follows:

opcode i,m

where *m* is a symbolic address (a label within the microprogram) and *i* is an integer between 0 and 23. This number specifies a bit within the register MDR or IR (depending on the opcode) which will be tested for zero. If this condition is satisfied the microprogram branches to the microinstruction labeled *m*; otherwise, execution continues with the next microinstruction following the branch instruction. In the case of an unconditional branch instruction, the operand *i* is omitted since no bit is tested.

With any branch instruction, the address must be a label within the microprogram supplied by the user; it is not allowed to reference any labels within the existing interpreter (appendix F). The only exception is the label FETCH, which marks the beginning of the fetch cycle. This label must be branched to at the end of each execution cycle. (Section 7.2 explains how a new microprogram segment supplied by the user is connected to the existing interpreter.)

5.2 THE ADD INSTRUCTION

The instruction ADD is the most frequently used instruction of the microprogramming language. It is used to compute the sum of two register contents. It is also used for 'moving' a value from one register to another by adding a zero to it and storing the result into the desired register. This is the only way to perform a register transfer operation, since no direct connections among registers exist in the MICOS architecture.

ADD in1,in2,out;shiftop;memop

This microinstruction causes the contents of the registers specified as "in1" and "in2" to be gated into the ALU/SHIFTER unit, where the values are added. The result is gated into the register specified as "out".

When the operand "shiftop" is present, the sum is shifted left or right before it is gated into the register "out", as discussed above.

Independent of "shiftop", the operand "memop" may be present, specifying a memory read or write operation.

The following examples illustrate the effect of the various operand combinations.

Example 5.1

```
ADD   MDR,A,A
```

The contents of the registers MDR and A are added in the ALU and the sum is gated into the register A, overwriting A's previous content. No shift or memory operation is performed.

Example 5.2

```
ADD   MDR,A,A;SHL
```

As in the previous example, the contents of the registers MDR and A are added in the ALU. Since the operand SHL is present, the sum is left-shifted by one bit before being gated into the register A.

Example 5.3:

```
a)   ADD   MDR,A,A;R
b)   ADD   MDR,A,A;SHL;R
```

Assume that the content of MAR is an integer n. In both cases, a) and b), the contents of MDR and A are added in the ALU. The sum, unchanged in the case a) and left-shifted by one in the case b), is gated into A. Independently of these operations, the content of the memory location n is copied into MDR, overwriting its previous value.

Example 5.4

```
ADD   STK,0,MAR;R
```

This instruction gates the contents of register STK and the constant 0 into the ALU. The result of the addition, which points to the top of the stack, is gated into MAR and the corresponding word is read. Hence the above instruction causes the current top-of-stack value to be read from memory into the register MDR.

If the operand SHL or SHR were specified with the above instruction, the stack pointer would be shifted left or right before being placed into MAR.

Example 5.5

ADD STK,0,MAR;W

This instruction is analogous to that of example 5.4; the stack pointer STK is moved to MAR and a write operation is performed. This causes the *top-of-stack* value to be overwritten with the current content of register MDR.

Example 5.6

ADD AUX,OPR,MDR;W

This instruction causes the contents of the registers AUX and OPR to be added and the result to be moved to MDR. Thereafter, a memory write operation is performed which transfers the new content of MDR into the memory location addressed by the current content of the register MAR.

5.3 THE UNCONDITIONAL BRANCH INSTRUCTION

```
┌─────────────┐
│             │
│             │
│    BR M     │
│             │
│             │
└─────────────┘
```

This microinstruction performs an unconditional branch to the microinstruction labeled M. Note that no gates will be opened during a branch instruction, and hence no data will flow between memory, the ALU/SHIFTER unit, or any registers.

Example 5.7 Write the execution cycle for the machine instruction ADD assuming that the interpreter branches to the label ADD whenever it fetches the machine instruction ADD.

As outlined in chapter 4, the execution cycle of any instruction must be terminated by a branch to the beginning of the fetch cycle. Assume that the first instruction of the fetch cycle is labeled FETCH.

```
ADD    ADD    STK,0,MAR;R
       ADD    MDR,0,AUX
       ADD    STK,1,STK
       ADD    STK,0,MAR;R
       ADD    MDR,AUX,MDR;W
       BR     FETCH
```

The first instruction causes the *tos*-value (*x*) to be read into MDR by gating the stack pointer STK into MAR and issuing a memory read operation. This is illustrated in figure 5.1a.

The second instruction moves the content of MDR into the auxiliary register AUX to free the register MDR for the next read operation (figure 5.1b).

The third instruction increments the stack pointer STK to reflect the new length of the stack, which must be shortened by one for the machine instruction ADD (recall that the stack "grows" toward address zero; see figure 5.1c).

The fourth instruction copies the contents of STK into MAR and causes the current *tos*-value (*y*) to be read into MDR (figure 5.1d).

At this point, both operands for the machine instruction ADD have been fetched and reside in the registers AUX and MDR. The fifth microinstruction

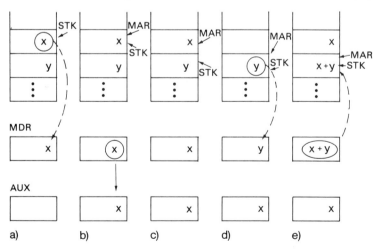

Figure 5.1

adds these two values, storing the result in MDR. The register MAR contains the value of STK from the previous read, thus a memory write operation causes the new value of MDR to be placed on the stack overwriting the value *y* (figure 5.1e). This value becomes the new *tos*-value. Note that the old *tos*-value *x* is not erased from memory; however, it is inaccessible by any subsequent machine instruction since the stack pointer has been incremented.

The last instruction is the unconditional branch to the label FETCH, which is the beginning of the fetch cycle where the next machine instruction will be fetched from memory. This branch occurs after the execution cycle of any machine instruction (except HALT).

5.4 THE SUBTRACT INSTRUCTION

> **SUB in1,in2,out;shiftop;memop**

This instruction performs a subtract operation in a way analogous to the instruction ADD. The content of the register "in2" is subtracted from the content of the register "in1" and the result is gated into the register specified as "out". As with the micro instruction ADD, the two optional operands "shiftop" and "memop" may be specified.

Example 5.8   Write the execution cycle for the machine instruction LDI assuming that the interpreter will branch to the label LDI whenever the instruction LDI is fetched. Assume further that during the fetch cycle the interpreter has placed the operand of the machine instruction (the constant *c* to be loaded on the stack) into the register OPR.

```
LDI   ADD   OPR,0,MDR
      SUB   STK,1,STK
      ADD   STK,0,MAR;W
      BR    FETCH
```

The first instruction transfers the operand (*c*) from OPR to MDR (figure 5.2a).

The second instruction decrements the stack pointer by subtracting the constant 1 from STK (figure 5.2b).

At this point STK points to the location of the new top-of-stack into which the content of MDR is transferred by moving STK to MAR and issuing a memory write operation (figure 5.2c).

The interpretation is terminated by a branch to the fetch cycle.

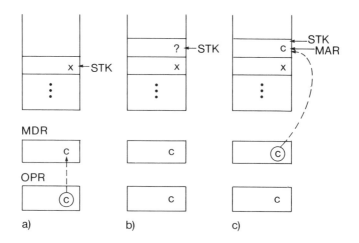

Figure 5.2

5.5 USING 12-BIT VERSUS 24-BIT REGISTERS

In the MICOS architecture (figure 4.1), registers of two different lengths—12 and 24 bits—can be distinguished. Since the input as well as the output registers of the ALU/SHIFTER unit may be of either length, the following rules are applied when ADD or SUB microinstructions are performed.

Input Registers

The value in any 12-bit input register is extended to 24 bits by padding the 12 left-most bits with the current sign bit: if the number in the 12-bit register is positive or zero then the 24-bit number is padded with 12 zeros, otherwise it is padded with 12 ones.

Output Registers

A 24-bit register can hold an integer in the range between -8388608 and $+8388607$. An ADD/SUB instruction may produce results which lie outside of this range and thus cannot be stored in a 24-bit register. If this is the case an error will occur and the computation will be aborted.

A 12-bit register can hold an integer in the range of -2048 and $+2047$. As opposed to a 24-bit register, an attempt to store a number outside of the legal range does not cause an error; rather, the number is truncated by discarding all but the 12 right-most bits.

This implementation allows, for example, the operand field of an instruction to be extracted simply by transferring the 24-bit instruction into a 12-bit register:

```
ADD   IR,0,MAR
```

This instruction causes the right-most 12 bits (the operand field) of the 24-bit register IR to be transferred to the 12-bit register MAR.

Note: The above rules are applied by the ALU independently of any subsequent shift operation performed by the SHIFTER. Thus, for example, when a value outside of the 24-bit range is produced by the ALU, an error will occur even if a right-shift operation (dividing the value by 2) is specified within the same microinstruction.

Example 5.9 Assume the registers MDR and AUX contain the following (binary) values:

```
MDR:   0111 1111 1111 1111 1111 1110
AUX:   0000 0000 0000 0000 0000 0011
```

The instruction

```
ADD   MDR,AUX,IN
```

produces the result 1000 ... 0001, which is greater than the maximum value $+8388607$. Since the output register is of length 24, an error will result.

Example 5.10 Assuming the same value for MDR and AUX as in example 5.9, consider the instruction

```
ADD   MDR,AUX,MAR
```

Since the output register MAR is of length 12, the sum produced by the ADD instruction is truncated to 12 bits, resulting in the value 0000 0000 0001, and stored in the register MAR. No error is reported.

Example 5.11 Assume the registers OPR and AUX contain the following (binary) values:

```
OPR:                         1000 0000 0001
AUX:      1000 0000 0000 0000 0000 0001
```

When the instruction

```
ADD   OPR,MDR,IN
```

is executed, the value OPR is extended by 12 leading ones and the addition is performed, resulting in a value less than − 8388608. Since the output register is of length 24, an error will occur.

Example 5.12 Assume the same values for OPR and MDR as in example 5.11. In the following instruction

```
ADD   OPR,MDR,MAR
```

the output register is of length 12. Hence the sum is truncated to 12 bits, resulting in the value 1000 0000 0010 stored in the register MAR.

5.6 LOGICAL GATE INSTRUCTIONS

```
AND  in1,in2,out;shiftop;memop
OR   in1,in2,out;shiftop;memop
EOR  in1,in2,out;shiftop;memop
```

Each of these instructions gates the content of the registers designated as "in1" and "in2" to the ALU where, depending on the opcode, the logical AND, logical OR, or Exclusive OR operation is performed. The result is gated into the register specified as "out."

As with the previous microinstructions ADD or SUB, the optional operands "shiftop" and/or "memop" may be specified.

Example 5.13 Each of the above three microinstructions is used to implement the corresponding machine instruction AND, OR, and EOR, respectively. The execution cycle of these instructions is analogous to that of ADD presented in section 5.2; the only distinction is in the microinstruction

```
ADD MDR,AUX,MDR;W
```

which performs the actual operation on the two operands. The opcode of this instruction must be replaced by AND, OR, and EOR, in order to implement the respective machine instructions (see appendix F).

Example 5.14 Write the execution cycle for the instruction COMP which performs the one's complement on the current *tos*-value.

```
COMP   ADD   STK,0,MAR;R
       EOR   MDR,-1,MDR;W
       BR    FETCH
```

The first instruction reads the current *tos*-value into MDR.

The second instruction complements the content of MDR and writes the result back into the same memory location. To understand how the complement operation is accomplished, consider the binary representation of the constant -1, which is a sequence of 24 ones. As discussed in section 2.7, the Exclusive OR of any bit with the digit 1 complements the value of that bit, thus the Exclusive OR of MDR with -1 causes all bits in MDR to be complemented.

Using 12-bit Versus 24-bit Registers with Logical Gate Instructions

For all logical microinstructions, the same rules as those given in section 5.5 for arithmetic microinstructions apply, that is,

- values in 12-bit registers are extended to 24 bits by extending their sign-bit,
- in case the output register is of length 12, the result is truncated by discarding the left-most 12 bits.

Note that none of the logical operations can ever produce a result which is outside of the range of legal integers, thus an error will never occur.

Example 5.15 Consider the instruction

```
OR   OPR,0,OUT
```

Assuming that the 12-bit register OPR contains the value -1 (in binary 1111 1111 1111), after execution of the instruction the 24-bit register OUT will also contain the value -1 (in binary 1111 1111 1111 1111 1111 1111), i.e. the sign bit of the number in the register OPR has been extended.

5.7 CONDITIONAL BRANCH INSTRUCTIONS

The following two conditional branch instructions exist in the microprogramming language:

BMDR i,M (*b*ranch on bit i of *MDR*)
BRIR   i,m (*b*ranch on bit i of *IR*)

In the case of BMDR, the *i*-th bit of the register MDR is tested. If that bit is zero a branch to the microinstruction labeled M is performed; otherwise, execution continues with the microinstruction immediately following BMDR. The number *i* may range from 0 to 23, where 23 is the left-most bit (the sign-bit).

The instruction BRIR is analogous to BMDR; instead of testing the *i*-th bit of the register MDR, the *i*-th bit of the instruction register IR is tested. This instruction is used mainly during the fetch cycle to determine the values of the index bit, the indirection bit, and the opcode of the machine instruction fetched for execution. (See appendix F and section 5.9.)

Example 5.16 Write the execution cycle for the instruction BPL M, which branches to the location M if the current *tos*-value is greater than or equal to zero.

```
BPL   ADD   STK,0,MAR;R
      BMDR  23,BR
      BR    FETCH
BR    ADD   OPR,0,PC
      BR    FETCH
```

The first instruction reads the *tos*-value into MDR; the second instruction then tests the sign-bit (bit 23) of MDR. If that bit is zero, which means that the value is greater than or equal to zero, a branch to the label BR is performed. There, the branch address M of the machine instruction BPL is placed into PC and a branch to the fetch cycle is performed. (Recall that OPR always contains the operand of the instruction being interpreted.) Since the program counter PC has been loaded with M, the next machine instruction will be fetched from memory location M, hence a branch to M at the machine level has been accomplished.

If the sign-bit of MDR is one, execution continues with the micro-instruction following BMDR, which is an unconditional branch to the fetch cycle. The PC register has not been altered by the execution cycle and hence no branch at the machine level takes place.

5.8 THE HALT INSTRUCTION

```
 ┌──────────────┐
 │              │
 │     HALT     │
 │              │
 └──────────────┘
```

This microinstruction causes the interpreter to cease execution; it is used to implement the machine instruction HALT.

5.9 THE FETCH CYCLE OF THE MICOS INTERPRETER

The function of the fetch cycle is to retrieve instructions from memory, determine their opcodes, and branch to the corresponding execution cycle to interpret the fetched instruction. In addition, the index and indirect address calculations are performed during the fetch cycle.

The fetch cycle is organized as follows (refer to appendix F):

- The instruction pointed to by the current value of PC is read from memory and transferred to the register IR.
- The value of PC is incremented by one to point to the next instruction.
- The operand field of the fetched instruction is copied to the register OPR.
- Bit 17 of IR is tested for zero; this bit distinguishes zero-operand and one-operand instructions (see list of opcodes in appendix A). If the bit 17 is equal to one, no operand is needed and hence the interpreter continues with a sequence of BRIR and BR instructions to determine the opcode of the fetched instruction. This sequence, referred to as *decoding* of the opcode, tests successively the opcode bits 16 through 12. When the opcode is determined, the interpreter branches to the appropriate execution cycle.

The decoding sequence follows the decision tree shown in figure 5.3, where each diamond-shaped box represents the test of one of the bits 16 through 12 of the IR register.

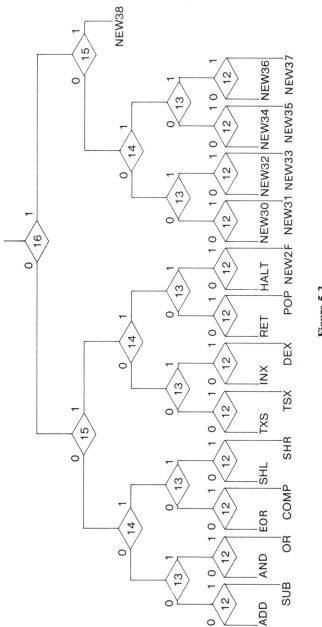

Figure 5.3

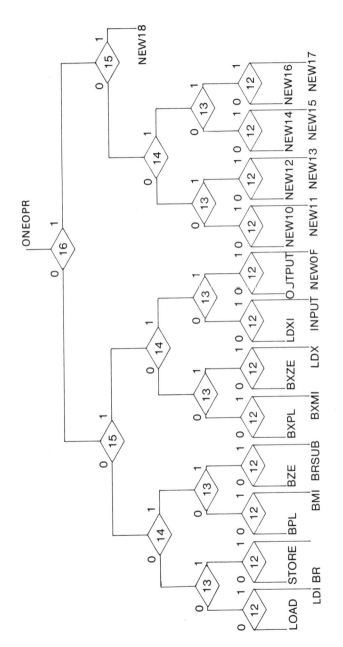

Figure 5.4

If the bit 17 is zero, indicating a one-operand instruction, the interpreter performs the actual address calculation as follows:

If the index bit is 1, the current content of the index register X is added to the operand in OPR.

If the indirection bit is 1, the interpreter uses the value in OPR as a memory address and reads the corresponding memory word. The indirection bit of that word is tested and if it is 1, the indirect address calculation is repeated. That is, the operand of the newly read word is used as a memory address and a read is performed. This sequence is repeated until the indirection bit is found to be zero. At that point, the address calculation is considered completed and the interpreter proceeds with the decoding sequence for one-operand instructions to determine the opcode of the instruction fetched. The decoding tree corresponding to this sequence is shown in figure 5.4.

Chapter 6

TRANSLATION OF MICROPROGRAMS

The microinstructions presented in section 5 constitute the *symbolic* microprogramming language. This language is provided only to facilitate the development of microprograms, as was the case with the assembly language discussed in part I. In order to be executed, a symbolic microprogram must be translated into a corresponding *numeric* microprogram. Each symbolic microinstruction is translated directly into its numeric equivalent which, depending on its type, has one of the following two formats:

a) Gate Instruction

23–20	19–16	15–12	11–8	7–4	3–0
opcode	in1	in2	out	shiftop	memop

b) Branch Instruction

23–20	19–12	11–0
opcode	i	address

The translation of microinstructions comprises the following tasks:

- Each symbolic opcode is translated into its numeric equivalent using table 6.1.
- Each of the symbolic operands *in1*, *in2*, and *out* is translated directly into its numeric equivalent using table 6.2.
- The operands "shiftop" and "memop" are translated into their numeric equivalents using the tables 6.3 and 6.4, respectively.
- The (decimal) number i, representing the bit to be tested, is converted into its two-digit hexadecimal equivalent 00 through 17. In the case of the un-

67

conditional branch BR, this field is 00.
- The symbolic branch address M is converted to the hexadecimal number corresponding to the micro-memory address of the instruction labeled M.

Table 6.1

Opcodes

Mnemonic	Code (hex)	Code (binary)
ADD	0	0000
SUB	1	0001
AND	2	0010
OR	3	0011
EOR	4	0100
BR	5	0101
BMDR	6	0110
BRIR	7	0111
HALT	8	1000

Table 6.2

Input/Output Registers (in1,in2,out)

Mnemonic	Code (hex)	Code (binary)
0	0	0000
1	1	0001
−1	2	0010
MDR	3	0011
IR	4	0100
X	5	0101
AUX	6	0110
IN	7	0111
OUT	8	1000
MAR	9	1001
OPR	A	1010
STK	B	1011
PC	C	1100

Table 6.3

Shift Operation (shiftop)

Mnemonic	Code (hex)	Code (binary)
(omitted)	0	0000
SHL	1	0001
SHR	2	0010

Table 6.4

Memory operation (memop)

Mnemonic	Code (hex)	Code (binary)
(omitted)	0	0000
R	1	0001
W	2	0010

Example 6.1 The translation of the symbolic microinstruction

            EOR   0,X,MDR;R

results in the numeric equivalent:

| 0100 | 0000 | 0101 | 0011 | 0000 | 0001 |

Example 6.2 The translation of the branch instruction

            BMDR   19,L1

results in the following numeric equivalent (we have assumed that the label L1 corresponds to the micro-memory location 1A).

| 0110 | 0001 | 0011 | 0000 | 0001 | 1010 |

PART III

Using the MICOS System

Chapter 7

SYSTEMS ORGANIZATION
AND CONTROL

The MICOS system consists of three programs, A, I, and M, and nine files, PROG, MPROG, OBJ, MOBJ, LIST, MLIST, DATA, RES, and NEWOP, used by these programs.* The overall structure of the system is shown in figure 7.1.

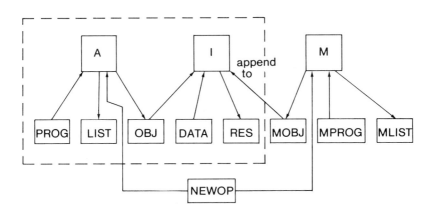

Figure 7.1

The user at the assembly language level is conerned only with the programs A and I, and the files PROG, LIST, OBJ, DATA, and RES. This subsystem is shown encircled by a dashed line in figure 7.1

---

*Depending on the computing facility running the MICOS system, the program names as well as the names of the files used by the programs may be modified by an extension, e.g. A.RUN or PROG.TEXT, as required by the facility.

7.1 USING THE ASSEMBLY LANGUAGE LEVEL ONLY

The program named A is the *assembler*. It reads the file PROG, which must contain an assembly language program, and it produces the two files LIST and OBJ.

The file LIST contains the *program listing,* which shows the assembly program as submitted in PROG and its translation into machine language, called the object code.

The file OBJ contains the machine language program (the object code) only. This file is used by the interpreter to execute the program.

Note: The machine language program in OBJ is internally encoded and should not be consulted by the programmer. In order to examine the machine program in its proper hexadecimal form only the listing file LIST should be used.

The program named I is the *interpreter*; it interprets the machine language program generated and placed into the file OBJ by the assembler.

The file DATA is the program *input file*; it contains the input values for the program being interpreted (see section 2.9).

The file RES is the *output file*; any result, including error messages, generated by the program during its execution are written into the file RES (see section 2.9).

Note: Copies of the files LIST and RES are automatically output to the user terminal for convenience reasons.

Sequence of Steps in Using the Assembly Language Level

1. Initial step: create two empty files called NEWOP and MOBJ. Even though the purpose of these files is of no concern to the user at the assembly language level, they must exist prior to executing the programs A and I, respectively; otherwise an error will occur.
2. Create the file PROG containing an assembly language program.
3. Execute the assembler A.

    Note: The command to run this program is machine dependent and must be supplied by the course instructor or the systems administrator; on most machines it will have one of the forms "RUN A," "R A," or simply "A."
4. Inspect the program listing (file LIST or the current terminal output). If errors were detected (see appendix D for the listing format and appendix E for a summary of error messages), then correct these and return to step 3; otherwise, continue with step 5.
5. Create the file DATA containing all input values to be read by the program submitted in the file PROG.

Note: The file DATA must exist even if no input values are to be read by the program; in this case the file will be empty.

6. Execute the interpreter I. Similar to step 3, the command to run this program is machine dependent and must be supplied by the course instructor or the systems administrator.

   After completion of I, all program outputs, including possible error messages, may be inspected in the file RES.

Example 7.1   Write a program which reads 5 integers from the input file DATA, finds the largest of these, and outputs it.

Step 1: Create two empty files called NEWOP and MOBJ.

Step 2: Write the assembly language program into the file PROG as shown in figure 7.2

```
* PROGRAM TO FIND THE MAXIMUM OF 5 INTEGERS
        LDXI    4           **PRESET X TO 5 ITERAT.
NEXTIN  INPUT   A,X         **READ 5 NUMBERS
        DEX                 *INTO ARRAY A
        BXPL    NEXTIN
        LDXI    4           **PRESET X TO 5 ITERAT.
        LOAD    A,X         **MAKE LAST EL. OF A TO
        STORE   MAX         *CURRENT MAX
NEXTNO  DEX                 **IF ALL ELEMENTS
        BXMI    OUTPUT      *PROCESSED-OUTPUT MAX
        LOAD    MAX         **COMPARE MAX TO
        LOAD    A,X         *CURR. EL. OF A
        SUB                 *
        BPL     NEXTNO      *IF MAX GREATER-CONT.
        LOAD    A,X         *ELSE OVERWRITE MAX
        STORE   MAX         *WITH CURR.EL. OF A
        BR      NEXTNO      **REPEAT FOR NEXT EL.
OUTPUT  OUTPUT  MAX
        HALT
A       BLOCK   5           **ARRAY A
MAX     BLOCK   1           **CURRENT MAXIMUM
```

Figure 7.2

Steps 3 and 4: Execute the assembler and inspect the listing for errors (figure 7.3).

```
LN   LOC   OBJECT   SOURCE-PROGRAM
---------------------------------
 1                  * PROGRAM TO FIND THE MAXIMUM OF 5 INTEGERS
 2   000   00C004            LDXI    4          **PRESET X TO 5 ITERAT.
 3   001   10D012   NEXTIN   INPUT   A,X        **READ 5 NUMBERS
 4   002   02B000            DEX                *INTO ARRAY A
 5   003   008001            BXPL    NEXTIN
 6   004   00C004            LDXI    4          **PRESET X TO 5 ITERAT.
 7   005   100012            LOAD    A,X        **MAKE LAST EL. OF A TO
 8   006   002017            STORE   MAX        *CURRENT MAX
 9   007   02B000   NEXTNO   DEX                **IF ALL ELEMENTS
10   008   009010            BXMI    OUTPUT     *PROCESSED-OUTPUT MAX
11   009   000017            LOAD    MAX        **COMPARE MAX TO
12   00A   100012            LOAD    A,X        *CURR. EL. OF A
13   00B   021000            SUB                *
14   00C   004007            BPL     NEXTNO     *IF MAX GREATER-CONT.
15   00D   100012            LOAD    A,X        *ELSE OVERWRITE MAX
16   00E   002017            STORE   MAX        *WITH CURR.EL. OF A
17   00F   003007            BR      NEXTNO     **REPEATE FOR NEXT EL.
18   010   00E017   OUTPUT   OUTPUT  MAX
19   011   02E000            HALT
20   012   000000   A        BLOCK   5          **ARRAY A
21   017   000000   MAX      BLOCK   1          **CURRENT MAXIMUM

*** ASSEMBLY COMPLETED ***
  0  ERRORS DETECTED
```

Figure 7.3

Step 5: Create the file DATA containing 5 test values (figure 7.4).

DATA

3 -4 50 0 27

Figure 7.4

Step 6: Execute the interpreter and inspect the file RES for output (figure 7.5).

```
PROGRAM OUTPUT:        50

*** EXECUTION COMPLETED ***
```

Figure 7.5

7.2 USING THE ASSEMBLY AND MICROPROGRAMMING LEVEL

The program named M is the *microprogram translator* (see figure 7.1); it reads the file MPROG, which contains the new segments of microcode written in the symbolic microprogramming language, and it produces the files MLIST and MOBJ.

Analogous to the file LIST, the file MLIST contains the microprogram listing which shows the symbolic microprogram as supplied in the file MPROG, and its translation into the numeric microcode, called the micro-object code.

The file MOBJ contains the micro-object code only; this code is automatically appended to the current interpreter I.

Note: As was the case with the file OBJ, the file MOBJ contains an internally encoded representation of the micro-object and should not be consulted by the programmer. To study the microprogram translation in its proper hexadecimal form only the file MLIST should be used.

As discussed in part II of this handbook, for each new assembly/machine instruction to be implemented a segment of microcode, representing its execution cycle, must be provided. The file MPROG contains the collection of all new execution cycles. In order to create the necessary links between the existing interpreter and the new execution cycles, the following conventions must be obeyed:

- Each new execution cycle must begin with a label which matches the symbolic opcode of the instruction it implements. For example, when a new assembly instruction MULT is being implemented, the corresponding segment of microcode must begin with the label MULT.
- The execution cycle of any instruction must end with the branch to the fetch cycle, BR FETCH.

(**Note:** No other label of the original interpreter but FETCH may be referenced by the new microprogram.)

For each new instruction being implemented, the new symbolic opcode must be supplied to the assembler A as well as to the microprogram translator M. The assembler needs this information to be able to translate symbolic opcodes into their numeric equivalents. The microprogram translator needs this information to be able to associate the branch labels NEW0F through NEW18 and NEW2F through NEW38 (see figures 5.3 and 5.4) with the addresses of the new microcode segments appended to the interpreter.

The new opcodes are supplied to the programs by the user in the file NEWOP, consisting of two lines. The first line contains a list of at most ten new opcodes, each representing a new one-operand instruction. The assembler reads this line and assigns to each symbolic opcode the numeric (hexadecimal) equivalents 0F through 18. Note that this sequence is the continuation of the sequence of opcodes 00 through 0E, each of which represents a one-operand instruction (see appendix A). In case no one-operand instruction is to be implemented, the first line of NEWOP must be blank.

The second line of NEWOP contains a list of at most ten new opcodes, each representing a new zero-operand instruction. The assembler reads this line and assigns to each symbolic opcode the numeric (hexadecimal) equivalent 2F through 38. This sequence is the continuation of the sequence of opcodes 20 through 2E, each representing a zero-operand instruction (see appendix A).

The microprogram translator uses the same file NEWOP to obtain the necessary information about the new opcode. It reads both lines and associates the labels NEW0F through NEW18 with the opcodes of the first line and the labels NEW2F through NEW38 with the opcodes of the second line. This guarantees that the interpreter branches to the correct new execution cycle for each new opcode.

Sequence of Steps in Using the Microprogramming Level

1. Create the file NEWOP containing the symbolic opcodes of all new assembly language instructions to be implemented. Line 1 of NEWOP must contain opcodes for all one-operand instructions, line 2 must contain opcodes for all zero-operand instructions.
2. Create a file MPROG which contains the execution cycles for each new instruction to be implemented. The starting label of each of these segments must match the symbolic opcode of the corresponding instruction listed in NEWOP. Each segment must end with the instruction BR FETCH.
3. Run the microprogram translator M. As was the case with A and I, the exact format of the command is machine dependent and must be supplied by the course instructor or the systems administrator.
4. Inspect the microprogram listing in the file MLIST (or on the terminal). If errors were detected (see appendixes D and E), correct these and return to step 3; otherwise, continue with step 5.
5. At this point the interpreter has been extended by the new microcode of MOBJ produced by M. To test the extended interpreter perform steps 2–6 of section 7.1, that is, create a test program (PROG) containing the new instructions, assemble it (using A), create the input file (DATA), and run the interpreter (I). The results of the program execution may be inspected in the file RES.

Example 7.6 Implement the following two new instructions:
    1) ADX
This instruction should add the current *tos*-value to the content of the index register X. The result should be placed into X and the *tos*-value should be removed from the stack.
    2) POPN n

This instruction should remove the *n* top-most elements from the stack.

Step 1: Create the file NEWOP (figure 7.6); line 1 must contain the opcode POPN while line 2 must contain the opcode ADX.

NEWOP

```
POPN
ADX
```

Figure 7.6

Step 2: Create the file MPROG containing the execution cycles for POPN and ADX (figure 7.7).

```
ADX      ADD     STK,0,MAR;R
         ADD     STK,1,STK
         ADD     X,MDR,X
         BR      FETCH
POPN     ADD     OPR,0,MDR
NXTPOP   BMDR    23,POP1
         BR      FETCH
POP1     ADD     STK,1,STK
         SUB     MDR,1,MDR
         BR      NXTPOP
```

Figure 7.7

Steps 3 and 4: Execute the microprogram translator M and inspect the listing for errors (figure 7.8).

```
LN  LOC  OBJECT  SOURCE-PROGRAM
-----------------------------------
 1   00  0B0901  ADX     ADD     STK,0,MAR;R
 2   01  0B1B00          ADD     STK,1,STK
 3   02  053500          ADD     X,MDR,X
 4   03  5000FF          BR      FETCH
 5   04  0A0300  POPN    ADD     OPR,0,MDR
 6   05  617007  NXTPOP  BMDR    23,POP1
 7   06  5000FF          BR      FETCH
 8   07  0B1B00  POP1    ADD     STK,1,STK
 9   08  131300          SUB     MDR,1,MDR
10   09  500005          BR      NXTPOP

*** MICRO ASSEMBLY COMPLETED ***
     0  ERRORS DETECTED
```

Figure 7.8

Step 5: Test the new instruction. Write a test program in PROG, assemble it (figure 7.9), and execute it (figure 7.10).

```
LN   LOC   OBJECT   SOURCE-PROGRAM
---------------------------------
 1                     * TEST PROGRAM FOR NEW INSTRUCTIONS ADX AND POPN
 2                     * IT SHOULD OUTPUT THE NUMBER 5 AND THEN PRODUCE
 3                     * THE ERROR: STACK IS EMPTY.
 4   000   00C003   TEST   LDXI    3
 5   001   001002          LDI     2
 6   002   02F000          ADX
 7   003   028000          TXS
 8   004   00200B          STORE   OUT
 9   005   00E00B          OUTPUT  OUT
10   006   00100A          LDI     10
11   007   00100B          LDI     11
12   008   00F002          POPN    2
13   009   00200B          STORE   OUT
14   00A   02E000          HALT
15   00B   000000   OUT    BLOCK   1
```

```
*** ASSEMBLY COMPLETED ***
  0  ERRORS DETECTED
```

Figure 7.9

```
PROGRAM OUTPUT:          5

******** ERROR AT ADDRESS 009 : STACK IS EMPTY
******** EXECUTION ABORTED ********
```

Figure 7.10

Chapter 8

TRACING OF PROGRAM EXECUTION

The MICOS system provides a debugging facility called *tracing* which allows the programmer to monitor the execution of individual instructions. Two pseudo instructions, TRACE and TREND (for *trace end*), are provided to designate a sequence of instructions for tracing. For each instruction enclosed between TRACE and TREND the interpreter will output additional information as an aid to the programmer to facilitate the task of program debugging.

A separate tracing facility exists for assembly language programs and microprograms; in both cases the same pseudo instructions TRACE and TREND are used.

8.1 TRACING AT THE ASSEMBLY LANGUAGE LEVEL

Any sequence of assembly language instructions enclosed between the pseudo instructions TRACE and TREND is designated for tracing. For each instruction within this sequence the system will output the current *tos*-value (in hexadecimal and decimal), the stack length (in decimal), and the content of the index register X (in hexadecimal and in decimal). This information has the following format:

```
*TRACE OF INSTRUCTION AT ADDRESS hexadr:
  TOS=hex1 (=    dec1)        STK.LENGTH=  len
    X=hex2 (=    dec2)
```

where
- "hexadr" is the hexadecimal location of the instruction being traced
- "hex1" and "dec1" are the current *tos*-value in hexadecimal and decimal, respectively
- "len" is the current stack length (in decimal)
- "hex2" and "dec2" are the current value of X in hexadecimal and decimal, respectively.

Note that the trace information is output *after* completion of each instruction execution, thus reflecting the changes performed by the instruction being traced.

Example 8.1   Trace the execution of the instruction SUB in the program of figure 7.2.

The pseudo instructions TRACE and TREND, respectively, are inserted before and after the instruction SUB and the program is assembled (figure 8.1).

```
LN   LOC   OBJECT   SOURCE-PROGRAM
------------------------------------
 1                        * PROGRAM TO FIND THE MAXIMUM OF 5 INTEGERS
 2   000   00C004               LDXI   4          **PRESET X TO 5 ITERAT.
 3   001   10D012    NEXTIN INPUT  A,X            **READ 5 NUMBERS
 4   002   02B000               DEX                *INTO ARRAY A
 5   003   008001               BXPL   NEXTIN
 6   004   00C004               LDXI   4          **PRESET X TO 5 ITERAT.
 7   005   100012               LOAD   A,X        **MAKE LAST EL. OF A TO
 8   006   002017               STORE  MAX         *CURRENT MAX
 9   007   02B000    NEXTNO DEX                    **IF ALL ELEMENTS
10   008   009010               BXMI   OUTPUT      *PROCESSED-OUTPUT MAX
11   009   000017               LOAD   MAX        **COMPARE MAX TO
12   00A   100012               LOAD   A,X         *CURR. EL. OF A
13                              TRACE
14   00B   021000               SUB                *
15                              TREND
16   00C   004007               BPL    NEXTNO      *IF MAX GREATER-CONT.
17   00D   100012               LOAD   A,X         *ELSE OVERWRITE MAX
18   00E   002017               STORE  MAX         *WITH CURR.EL. OF A
19   00F   003007               BR     NEXTNO     **REPEAT FOR NEXT EL.
20   010   00E017    OUTPUT OUTPUT MAX
21   011   02E000               HALT
22   012   000000    A      BLOCK  5              **ARRAY A
23   017   000000    MAX    BLOCK  1              **CURRENT MAXIMUM

*** ASSEMBLY COMPLETED ***
  0 ERRORS DETECTED
```

Figure 8.1

The program is executed producing the output as shown in figure 8.2. The trace information shows the changes in the current *tos*-value, the stack length, and the index register for each execution of the instruction at location 00B (see listing in figure 8.1).

```
    * TRACE OF INSTRUCTION AT ADDRESS 00B:
      TOS=000001 (=        1)        STK.LENGTH=          1
      X=000003 (=         3)

    * TRACE OF INSTRUCTION AT ADDRESS 00B:
      TOS=00000C (=       12)        STK.LENGTH=          2
      X=000002 (=         2)

    * TRACE OF INSTRUCTION AT ADDRESS 00B:
      TOS=FFFFD8 (=      -40)        STK.LENGTH=          3
      X=000001 (=         1)

    * TRACE OF INSTRUCTION AT ADDRESS 00B:
      TOS=000028 (=       40)        STK.LENGTH=          4
      X=000000 (=         0)
    PROGRAM OUTPUT:          50

    *** EXECUTION COMPLETED ***
```

Figure 8.2

8.2 TRACING AT THE MICROPROGRAMMING LEVEL

Any sequence of microinstructions enclosed between the pseudo instructions TRACE and TREND is designated for tracing. For each microinstruction within this sequence the system will output the following trace information:

```
**TRACE OF MICROINSTRUCTION AT MM.ADDRESS hexadr1
  (INTERPRETING MACHINE INSTRUCTION AT hexadr2)
  MDR    IR    X    AUX    MAR OPR STK PC
  hx1    hx2   hx3  hx4    hx5 hx6 hx7 hx8
```

where
• "hexadr1" is the hexadecimal location of the microinstruction being traced
• "hexadr2" is the hexadecimal location of the machine instruction currently being interpreted
• "hx1" through "hx8" are the current (hexadecimal) contents of the registers MDR, IR, X, AUX, MAR, OPR, STK, and PC, respectively.

As was the case with the trace information at the assembly language level, the trace information at the microprogramming level is output *after* completion of each microinstruction.

Example 8.2 Trace the microinstructions ADD and SUB within the microprogram for POPN.

The pseudo instructions TRACE and TREND are inserted into the microprogram and the microprogram translator M is executed, producing the listing shown in figure 8.3.

```
LN  LOC  OBJECT   SOURCE-PROGRAM
---------------------------------------
 1   00  0B0901   ADX      ADD      STK,0,MAR;R
 2   01  0B1B00            ADD      STK,1,STK
 3   02  053500            ADD      X,MDR,X
 4   03  5000FF            BR       FETCH
 5   04  0A0300   POPN     ADD      OPR,0,MDR
 6   05  617007   NXTPOP   BMDR     23,POP1
 7   06  5000FF            BR       FETCH
 8                         TRACE
 9   07  0B1B00   POP1     ADD      STK,1,STK
10   08  131300            SUB      MDR,1,MDR
11                         TREND
12   09  500005            BR       NXTPOP
```

```
*** MICRO ASSEMBLY COMPLETED ***
    0 ERRORS DETECTED
```

Figure 8.3

The interpreter I is restarted with the same program as that of section 7.2 (figure 7.9), producing the output shown in figure 8.4. This output shows the trace of the two instructions at micro-memory locations 07 and 08 (see figure 8.3), executed three times during the interpretation of the machine instruction at location 008 (see figure 7.9).

```
PROGRAM OUTPUT:            5

** TRACE OF MICROINSTRUCTION AT MM.ADDRESS 07
   (INTERPRETING MACHINE INSTRUCTION AT 008)
   MDR     IR       X       AUX      MAR OPR STK PC
   000002  00F002  000005  000000   008 002 1FF 009

** TRACE OF MICROINSTRUCTION AT MM.ADDRESS 08
   (INTERPRETING MACHINE INSTRUCTION AT 008)
   MDR     IR       X       AUX      MAR OPR STK PC
   000001  00F002  000005  000000   008 002 1FF 009

** TRACE OF MICROINSTRUCTION AT MM.ADDRESS 07
   (INTERPRETING MACHINE INSTRUCTION AT 008)
   MDR     IR       X       AUX      MAR OPR STK PC
   000001  00F002  000005  000000   008 002 200 009

** TRACE OF MICROINSTRUCTION AT MM.ADDRESS 08
   (INTERPRETING MACHINE INSTRUCTION AT 008)
   MDR     IR       X       AUX      MAR OPR STK PC
   000000  00F002  000005  000000   008 002 200 009

** TRACE OF MICROINSTRUCTION AT MM.ADDRESS 07
   (INTERPRETING MACHINE INSTRUCTION AT 008)
   MDR     IR       X       AUX      MAR OPR STK PC
   000000  00F002  000005  000000   008 002 201 009

** TRACE OF MICROINSTRUCTION AT MM.ADDRESS 08
   (INTERPRETING MACHINE INSTRUCTION AT 008)
   MDR     IR       X       AUX      MAR OPR STK PC
   FFFFFF  00F002  000005  000000   008 002 201 009

******** ERROR AT ADDRESS 009 : STACK IS EMPTY
******** EXECUTION ABORTED *********
```

Figure 8.4

Appendix A

INSTRUCTION SET OF THE ASSEMBLY LANGUAGE

One-Operand Instructions

code	instruction		stack length	description
00	LOAD	M	+1	Load stack from memory location M
01	LDI	c	+1	Load stack with constant c
02	STORE	M	−1	Store tos to memory location M
03	BR	M	0	Branch to location M
04	BPL	M	0	Branch to M if tos is > or = zero
05	BMI	M	0	Branch to M if tos is < zero
06	BZE	M	0	Branch to M if tos is = zero
07	BRSUB	M	+1	Branch to M and save return address on stack
08	BXPL	M	0	Branch to M if X is > or = zero
09	BXMI	M	0	Branch to M if X is < zero
0A	BXZE	M	0	Branch to M if X is = zero
0B	LDX	M	0	Load X from memory location M
0C	LDXI	c	0	Load X with constant c
0D	INPUT	M	0	Input value from file DATA to location M
0E	OUTPUT	M	0	Output value from location M to file RES

Zero-Operand Instructions

code	instruction	stack length	description
20	ADD	−1	Add 2 top-most values of stack
21	SUB	−1	Subtract tos from value next below tos
22	AND	−1	AND 2 top-most values of stack
23	OR	−1	OR 2 top-most values of stack
24	EOR	−1	Excl. OR 2 top-most values of stack
25	COMP	0	Complement tos (one's complement)
26	SHL	0	Shift left tos by one
27	SHR	0	Shift right tos by one
28	TXS	+1	Transfer X to tos
29	TSX	−1	Transfer tos to X
2A	INX	0	Increment X by one

2B	DEX	0	Decrement X by one
2C	RET	-1	Return from subroutine
2D	POP	-1	Discard tos
2E	HALT	0	Terminate execution

Pseudo Instructions

instruction	description
BLOCK n	Reserve n words of memory preset to zero
DATA c	Reserve 1 word preset to the decimal constant c
DATA X'h'	Reserve 1 word preset to the hexadecimal constant h
TRACE	Start trace
TREND	End trace

Appendix B

THE INSTRUCTION SET OF THE MICROPROGRAMMING LANGUAGE

Executable Instructions

code	instruction	description
0	ADD	ADD in1 to in2, store result in out
1	SUB	Subtract in1 from in2, store result in out
2	AND	AND in1 with in2, store result in out
3	OR	OR in1 with in2, store result in out
4	EOR	Excl. OR in1 with in2, store result in out
5	BR M	Branch to location M
6	BMDR i,M	Branch to location M if bit i of MDR is zero
7	BRIR i,M	Branch to location M if bit i of IR is zero
8	HALT	Terminate execution

Pseudo Instructions

instruction	description
TRACE	Start microprogram trace
TREND	End microprogram trace

Appendix C

THE MICOS INTERPRETER

```
LN  LOC  OBJECT  SOURCE-PROGRAM
-----------------------------------------------------------
 1  *** INTERPRETER FOR THE STANDARD MICOS INSTRUCT ON SET ***

 2  00   0C0901  FETCH    ADD    PC,0,MAR;R
 3  01   030400           ADD    MDR,0,IR
 4  02   0C1C00           ADD    PC,1,PC
 5  03   030A00           ADD    MDR,0,OPR
 6  04   166600           SUB    AUX,AUX,AUX
 7  05   71102B           BRIR   17,ONEOPR
 8  06   710014           BRIR   16,I2
 9  07   70F009           BRIR   15,I22
10  08   5000D7           BR     NEW38
11  09   70E00F  I22      BRIR   14,I221
12  0A   70D00D           BRIR   13,I2212
13  0B   70C0D5           BRIR   12,NEW36
14  0C   5000D6           BR     NEW37
15  0D   70C0D3  I2212    BRIR   12,NEW34
16  0E   5000D4           BR     NEW35
17  0F   70D012  I221     BRIR   13,I2211
18  10   70C0D1           BRIR   12,NEW32
19  11   5000D2           BR     NEW33
20  12   70C0CF  I2211    BRIR   12,NEW30
21  13   5000D0           BR     NEW31
22  14   70F020  I2       BRIR   15,I21
23  15   70E01B           BRIR   14,I212
24  16   70D019           BRIR   13,I2122
25  17   70C0C3           BRIR   12,HALT
26  18   5000CE           BR     NEW2F
27  19   70C0BD  I2122    BRIR   12,RET
28  1A   5000C1           BR     POP
29  1B   70D01E  I212     BRIR   13,I2121
30  1C   70C0B9           BRIR   12,INX
31  1D   5000BB           BR     DEX
32  1E   70C0B1  I2121    BRIR   12,TXS
33  1F   5000B5           BR     TSX
34  20   70E026  I21      BRIR   14,I211
35  21   70D024           BRIR   13,I2112
36  22   70C0AB           BRIR   12,SHL
37  23   5000AE           BR     SHR
38  24   70C0A2  I2112    BRIR   12,EOR
39  25   5000A8           BR     COMP
40  26   70D029  I211     BRIR   13,I2111
41  27   70C096           BRIR   12,AND
42  28   50009C           BR     OR
43  29   70C08A  I2111    BRIR   12,ADD
44  2A   500090           BR     SUB
45  2B   71402D  ONEOPR   BRIR   20,INDIR
46  2C   0A5A00           ADD    OPR,X,OPR
```

47	2D	715031	INDIR	BRIR	21,IXDONE
48	2E	0A0901		ADD	OPR,0,MAR;R
49	2F	030A00		ADD	MDR,0,OPR
50	30	50002D		BR	INDIR
51	31	71003F	IXDONE	BRIR	16,I1
52	32	70F034		BRIR	15,I12
53	33	5000CD		BR	NEW18
54	34	70E03A	I12	BRIR	14,I121
55	35	70D038		BRIR	13,I1212
56	36	70C0CB		BRIR	12,NEW16
57	37	5000CC		BR	NEW17
58	38	70C0C9	I1212	BRIR	12,NEW14
59	39	5000CA		BR	NEW15
60	3A	70D03D	I121	BRIR	13,I1211
61	3B	70C0C7		BRIR	12,NEW12
62	3C	5000C8		BR	NEW13
63	3D	70C0C7	I1211	BRIR	12,NEW12
64	3E	5000C6		BR	NEW11
65	3F	70F04B	I1	BRIR	15,I11
66	40	70E046		BRIR	14,I112
67	41	70D044		BRIR	13,I1122
68	42	70C087		BRIR	12,OUTPUT
69	43	5000C4		BR	NEW0F
70	44	70C082	I1122	BRIR	12,LDXI
71	45	500084		BR	INPUT
72	46	70D049	I112	BRIR	13,I1121
73	47	70C07C		BRIR	12,BXZE
74	48	50007F		BR	LDX
75	49	70C076	I1121	BRIR	12,BXPL
76	4A	500079		BR	BXMI
77	4B	70E051	I11	BRIR	14,I111
78	4C	70D04F		BRIR	13,I1112
79	4D	70C06A		BRIR	12,BZE
80	4E	500071		BR	BRSUB
81	4F	70C064	I1112	BRIR	12,BPL
82	50	500067		BR	BMI
83	51	70D054	I111	BRIR	13,I1111
84	52	70C05E		BRIR	12,STORE
85	53	500062		BR	BR
86	54	70C056	I1111	BRIR	12,LOAD
87	55	50005A		BR	LDI
88	56	0A0901	LOAD	ADD	OPR,0,MAR;R
89	57	1B1B00		SUB	STK,1,STK
90	58	0B0902		ADD	STK,0,MAR;W
91	59	500000		BR	FETCH
92	5A	0A0300	LDI	ADD	OPR,0,MDR
93	5B	1B1B00		SUB	STK,1,STK
94	5C	0B0902		ADD	STK,0,MAR;W
95	5D	500000		BR	FETCH
96	5E	0B0901	STORE	ADD	STK,0,MAR;R
97	5F	0A0902		ADD	OPR,0,MAR;W
98	60	0B1B00		ADD	STK,1,STK
99	61	500000		BR	FETCH
100	62	0A0C00	BR	ADD	OPR,0,PC
101	63	500000		BR	FETCH
102	64	0B0901	BPL	ADD	STK,0,MAR;R
103	65	617062		BMDR	23,BR
104	66	500000		BR	FETCH
105	67	0B0901	BMI	ADD	STK,0,MAR;R
106	68	617000		BMDR	23,FETCH
107	69	500062		BR	BR
108	6A	0B0901	BZE	ADD	STK,0,MAR;R
109	6B	61706D		BMDR	23,GRZERO
110	6C	500000		BR	FETCH

111	6D	432300	GRZERO	EOR	MDR,-1,MDR
112	6E	031300		ADD	MDR,1,MDR
113	6F	617062		BMDR	23,BR
114	70	500000		BR	FETCH
115	71	0C0300	BRSUB	ADD	PC,0,MDR
116	72	1B1B00		SUB	STK,1,STK
117	73	0B0902		ADD	STK,0,MAR;W
118	74	0A0C00		ADD	OPR,0,PC
119	75	500000		BR	FETCH
120	76	050300	BXPL	ADD	X,0,MDR
121	77	617062		BMDR	23,BR
122	78	500000		BR	FETCH
123	79	050300	BXMI	ADD	X,0,MDR
124	7A	617000		BMDR	23,FETCH
125	7B	500062		BR	BR
126	7C	050300	BXZE	ADD	X,0,MDR
127	7D	61706D		BMDR	23,GRZERO
128	7E	500000		BR	FETCH
129	7F	0A0901	LDX	ADD	OPR,0,MAR;R
130	80	030500		ADD	MDR,0,X
131	81	500000		BR	FETCH
132	82	0A0500	LDXI	ADD	OPR,0,X
133	83	500000		BR	FETCH
134	84	070300	INPUT	ADD	IN,0,MDR
135	85	0A0902		ADD	OPR,0,MAR;W
136	86	500000		BR	FETCH
137	87	0A0901	OUTPUT	ADD	OPR,0,MAR;R
138	88	030800		ADD	MDR,0,OUT
139	89	500000		BR	FETCH
140	8A	0B0901	ADD	ADD	STK,0,MAR;R
141	8B	030600		ADD	MDR,0,AUX
142	8C	0B1B00		ADD	STK,1,STK
143	8D	0B0901		ADD	STK,0,MAR;R
144	8E	036302		ADD	MDR,AUX,MDR;W
145	8F	500000		BR	FETCH
146	90	0B0901	SUB	ADD	STK,0,MAR;R
147	91	030600		ADD	MDR,0,AUX
148	92	0B1B00		ADD	STK,1,STK
149	93	0B0901		ADD	STK,0,MAR;R
150	94	136302		SUB	MDR,AUX,MDR;W
151	95	500000		BR	FETCH
152	96	0B0901	AND	ADD	STK,0,MAR;R
153	97	030600		ADD	MDR,0,AUX
154	98	0B1B00		ADD	STK,1,STK
155	99	0B0901		ADD	STK,0,MAR;R
156	9A	236302		AND	MDR,AUX,MDR;W
157	9B	500000		BR	FETCH
158	9C	0B0901	OR	ADD	STK,0,MAR;R
159	9D	030600		ADD	MDR,0,AUX
160	9E	0B1B00		ADD	STK,1,STK
161	9F	0B0901		ADD	STK,0,MAR;R
162	A0	336302		OR	MDR,AUX,MDR;W
163	A1	500000		BR	FETCH
164	A2	0B0901	EOR	ADD	STK,0,MAR;R
165	A3	030600		ADD	MDR,0,AUX
166	A4	0B1B00		ADD	STK,1,STK
167	A5	0B0901		ADD	STK,0,MAR;R
168	A6	436302		EOR	MDR,AUX,MDR;W
169	A7	500000		BR	FETCH
170	A8	0B0901	COMP	ADD	STK,0,MAR;R
171	A9	432302		EOR	MDR,-1,MDR;W
172	AA	500000		BR	FETCH
173	AB	0B0901	SHL	ADD	STK,0,MAR;R
174	AC	030312		ADD	MDR,0,MDR;SHL;W

```
175   AD   500000           BR     FETCH
176   AE   0B0901    SHR    ADD    STK,0,MAR;R
177   AF   030322           ADD    MDR,0,MDR;SHR;W
178   B0   500000           BR     FETCH
179   B1   1B1900    TXS    SUB    STK,1,MAR
180   B2   050302           ADD    X,0,MDR;W
181   B3   1B1B00           SUB    STK,1,STK
182   B4   500000           BR     FETCH
183   B5   0B0901    TSX    ADD    STK,0,MAR;R
184   B6   030500           ADD    MDR,0,X
185   B7   0B1B00           ADD    STK,1,STK

186   B8   500000           BR     FETCH
187   B9   051500    INX    ADD    X,1,X
188   BA   500000           BR     FETCH
189   BB   151500    DEX    SUB    X,1,X
190   BC   500000           BR     FETCH
191   BD   0B0901    RET    ADD    STK,0,MAR;R
192   BE   0B1B00           ADD    STK,1,STK
193   BF   030C00           ADD    MDR,0,PC
194   C0   500000           BR     FETCH
195   C1   0B1B00    POP    ADD    STK,1,STK
196   C2   500000           BR     FETCH
197   C3   800000    HALT   HALT
```

```
              *** MICRO ASSEMBLY COMPLETED ***
                   0   ERRORS DETECTED
```

Appendix D

SUMMARY OF FILE FORMATS

Files PROG/MPROG

Each line of the files PROG/MPROG may contain
* a comment starting with an asterisk in column 1, or
* an assembly/micro instruction in the following format:

    a. columns 1-6 : label (optional)
    b. column 7   : blank
    c. columns 8-13: opcode
    d. column 14 : blank
    e. columns 15-n: operands (optional), where n depends on the length and the
                           number of operands

Any instruction may be followed by a comment which must be separated by at least 5 blanks from the last character of the instruction.

File LIST/MLIST

Each of these files contains a listing header and a termination message showing the number of errors detected during assembly/translation. (For an example of LIST and MLIST, see figures 7.3 and 7.8, respectively.)
    The program listing between the header and the termination message consists of the following components:

* sequence of line numbers (header LN)
* memory locations for each instruction (header LOC)
* translation of source program (header OBJECT)
* assembly or micro program (header SOURCE PROGRAM)

File DATA

This file may contain any number of integers, each of which must be in the range between -8388608 and $+8388607$. These integers may be distributed over any number of lines. Each pair of integers on the same line must be separated by at least one blank from one another.

92

Example:

```
1 2 54      -5 11111
   45
-17 838867            15
```

File NEWOP

The first line of this file must contain 0 to 10 opcodes for new one-operand instructions; the second line must contain 0 to 10 opcodes for new zero-operand instructions.

Each opcode must be a string of 1 to 6 characters. All opcodes on the same line must be separated by at least one blank from one another.

Files OBJ/MOBJ

These files are used internally by the system and their format is of no significance to the programmer.

Initially, these files must be created as empty files.

Appendix E

ALPHABETICAL SUMMARY
OF ERROR MESSAGES

1. Error Messages Generated by the Assembler.

The following three error messages indicate a fatal error, causing the assembler to abort the assembly process:

NEW OPCODE IS TOO LONG

One of the new opcodes in the file NEWOP is longer than 6 characters.

NUMBER OF LABELS EXCEEDS 100

The assembly program contains more than 100 labels, which is the maximum that can be processed by the assembler.

PROGRAM EXCEEDS MEMORY SIZE 512

The machine program exceeds the available memory space of 512 words. Note that the machine program can be longer than the submitted assembly program because of the pseudo instruction BLOCK, which reserves n words of memory.

The following messages will be output following the instruction in error and the assembly process will proceed with the next instruction:

COLUMN 7 IS NOT BLANK

A non-blank character has been detected between the label and the opcode field.

COLUMN 15 IS NOT BLANK

A non-blank character has been detected between the opcode and the operand field.

ILLEGAL OPERAND

The operand field has an illegal format; it contains blanks, or its numerical value exceeds the maximum range allowed for that instruction.

LABEL DOES NOT BEGIN WITH A LETTER

Label does not begin with an alphabetical character A through Z.

LABEL OR COMMENT DOES NOT BEGIN IN COLUMN 1

The line begins with a blank followed by a non-blank character within the label field.

NO OPERAND ALLOWED

Operand field of zero-operand instructions and the pseudo instructions TRACE and TREND must be blank. In the case of a new opcode supplied via the file NEWOP, the opcode is on the wrong line (line 2) of NEWOP.

OPCODE DOES NOT BEGIN IN COLUMN 8

First character of opcode field is blank.

OPCODE IS ILLEGAL OR NOT FOLLOWED BY BLANKS

Opcode not recognized or the opcode filed contains non-blank characters following the actual opcode.

OPERAND IS MISSING OR NOT IN COLUMN 16

First character of operand field is blank; instruction requires operand. In the case of a new opcode supplied via the file NEWOP the opcode is on the wrong line (line 1) of NEWOP.

OPERAND IS TOO LARGE/SMALL

The numerical value of the operand is outside of the legal range for that instruction.

REFERENCE TO A MULTIPLY DEFINED LABEL

The operand contains a label which appears in front of more than one instruction within the program.

REFERENCE TO UNDEFINED LABEL

The operand contains a label which does not appear in front of any instruction within the program.

2. Error Messages Generated by the Interpreter

ASSEMBLY WAS NOT ERROR-FREE

A program may be executed only if no errors were detected by the assembler, otherwise no machine language program is generated.

DATA FILE IS EMPTY

The input file DATA contains fewer integers than requested by the program during execution; the program attempts to read past the last value.

LEFT-MOST 2 INSTRUCTION BITS ARE NOT ZERO

For any executable instruction, the assembler places zeros into the two left-most bits. This error can occur only if the interpreter attempts to execute a data constant which contains a one in one (or both) of the left-most bits (see section 3.3).

ILLEGAL MACHINE OPCODE

The assembler will generate only legal opcodes; this error can occur only if the interpreter attempts to execute a data constant in which the bits 19–12 (the opcode field) do not represent a legal machine opcode (see section 3.3).

INPUT CONTAINS ILLEGAL CHARACTERS

A character other than 0 through 9 has been found when reading a value from the input file DATA.

INPUT VALUE IS TOO LARGE/SMALL

The program attempts to read a value from the input file DATA which is outside of the legal range of -8388608 to $+8388607$.

INVALID MEMORY LOCATION

Program attempts to reference a non-existent memory location (less than 0 or greater than 511). This error may also occur when the HALT instruction is missing.

NO "BR FETCH" MICROINSTRUCTION ENCOUNTERED

One of the microprogram segments in MPROG does not end with the micro instruction BR FETCH.

NO HALT INSTRUCTION ENCOUNTERED

No HALT instruction was encountered, which causes the interpreter to continue execution past the last line of the program, interpreting all subsequent memory words (containing all zeros) as LOAD 0. This leads to one of the following cases: the last memory location 511 is reached (resulting in the above error message), or the stack grows past the location 0, in which case the error message INVALID MEMORY LOCATION is generated (see above).

RESULT IS TOO LARGE/SMALL
An arithmetic instruction generated a value outside of the legal range -8388608 to $+8388607$.

STACK IS EMPTY

An instruction attempts to reference the stack while it is empty. In the case of arithmetic or logical operations the stack must contain at least two values.

3. Error Messages Generated by the Microprogram Translator

The following four error messages indicate a fatal error, causing the translator to abort the translation process:

NEW OPCODE IS TOO LONG

One of the new opcodes in the file NEWOP is longer than 6 characters.

NO MICROPROGRAM FOR NEW OPCODE

The file MPROG does not contain the execution cycle for one of the new opcodes listed in the file NEWOP.

NUMBER OF LABELS EXCEEDS 20

The microprogram in MPROG contains more than 20 labels, which is the maximum number that can be processed by the translator.

PROGRAM EXCEEDS MEMORY SIZE 64

The microprogram exceeds the available memory space of 64 words.

The following messages will be output following the instruction in error and the translation process will proceed with the next instruction:

BIT NUMBER IS NOT WITHIN 0–23

The test bit specified with the instruction BMDR or BRIR must be an integer between 0 and 23.

COLUMN 7 IS NOT BLANK

A non-blank character has been detected between the label and the opcode field.

COLUMN 15 IS NOT BLANK

A non-blank character has been detected between the opcode and the operand field.

ILLEGAL OPERAND FORMAT

The operand field has an illegal format or contains blanks.

LABEL DOES NOT BEGIN WITH A LETTER

Label does not begin with an alphabetic character A through Z.

LABEL OR COMMENT DOES NOT BEGIN IN COLUMN 1

The line begins with a blank followed by a non-blank character within the label field.

OPCODE DOES NOT BEGIN IN COLUMN 8

First character of opcode field is blank

OPCODE IS ILLEGAL OR NOT FOLLOWED BY BLANKS

Opcode not recognized or the opcode filed contains non-blank characters following the actual opcode.

OPERAND IS MISSING OR NOT IN COLUMN 16

First character of operand field is blank.

OPERAND *i* IS ILLEGAL

The number *i* is an integer from 1 to 3, indicating an error in the operand in1, in2, or out, respectively; the register name does not exist or the register is not connected to the corresponding bus.

REFERENCE TO A MULTIPLY DEFINED LABEL

The operand contains a label which appears in front of more than one instruction within the program.

REFERENCE TO UNDEFINED LABEL

The operand contains a label which does not appear in front of any instruction within the program.

Appendix F

INTRODUCTION TO NUMBER SYSTEMS

F.1. POSITIVE INTEGERS

F.1.1 The Decimal Number System

A positive decimal integer d is represented as a sequence of digits $dn \ldots d2d1d0$, where each di can have one of the values 0 through 9. The meaning of each digit is as follows: $d0$ specifies the number of ones, $d1$ specifies the number of tens, $d2$ specifies the number of hundreds, etc. This can be expressed formally as follows:

$$d = d0*10^0 + d1*10^1 + d2*10^2 + \ldots + dn*10^n$$

The right-hand side of this expression is referred to as the *meaning* or the *interpretation* of the number d.

Example 1: The interpretation of the number 206 has the following form:

$$206 = 6*10^0 + 0*10^1 + 2*10^2$$
$$= 6*1 + 0*10 + 2*100$$

The number 10 used as the base for the exponentiation is called the *radix*. The choice of the radix determines how sequences of digits are interpreted, that is, it specifies the decimal value represented by a given sequence of digits. Thus each distinct radix defines a new number system. In this book we are concerned only with the radices 2, 10, and 16, which yield the *binary*, the *decimal*, and the *hexadecimal* number systems respectively.

F.1.2 Binary Numbers

A positive binary integer b is a sequence of digits $bn \ldots b2b1b0$, where each bi is referred to as a *binary digit* (bit) and can have the value 0 or 1. That is, the binary number system consists of only 2 digits, as opposed to 10 digits constituting the decimal number system.

The interpretation of a binary number b is expressed as follows:

$$b = b0*2^0 + b1*2^1 + b2*2^2 + \ldots + bn*2^n$$

When evaluated, the right-hand side of the expression yields the decimal value represented by the binary number $bn \ldots b0$.

Example 2:

$$11010 = 0*2^0 + 1*2^1 + 0*2^2 + 1*2^3 + 1*2^4$$

The right-hand side of the expression evaluates the decimal number 26, thus the sequence of digits 11010 in the binary system represents the same value as the sequence of digits 26 in the decimal system.

The first two columns of table F.1 show the first thirty-two decimal numbers and their binary equivalents.

F.1.3 Hexadecimal Numbers

A positive hexadecimal integer h is a sequence of digits $hn \ldots h2h1h0$ where each hi is referred to as a *hexadecimal unit*. There are 16 possible values, 0, 1, ..., 9, A, B, C, D, E, F, for each hexadecimal digit, where A corresponds to the decimal value 10, B corresponds to 11, etc.

The interpretation of a hexadecimal number h is expressed as follows:

$$h = h0*16^0 + h1*16^1 + h2*16^2 + \ldots + hn*16^n$$

The right-hand side of the above expression yields the decimal equivalent of the hexadecimal number $hn \ldots h0$.

Example 3:

$$1A3C = C*16^0 + 3*16^1 + A*16^2 + 1*16^3$$

The right-hand side of the expression evaluates to the decimal number 6716, thus, the sequence of digits 1A3C in the hexadecimal system represents the same value as the sequence of digits 6716 in the decimal system.

Column 3 of table F.1 shows the first thirty-two hexadecimal numbers.

Notation:

To distinguish numbers belonging to different number systems, the radix of the corresponding system is frequently attached to the number as a subscript. For example, 110_2 is a binary number (corresponding to 6 in decimal, i.e. 6_{10}), whereas 110_{16} is a hexadecimal number (corresponding to 272_{10}).

F.1.4 Number Conversions

This section discusses how to convert the representations of a number from one number system to the corresponding representation in another system.

Binary to Decimal Conversion

In section F.1.2, the interpretation of a binary number b has been defined as the sequence $b0*2^0 + \ldots + bn*2^n$, where each bi is a binary digit. The value of this expression yields a decimal value d corresponding to the binary number b. Thus, the procedure to convert a binary number b to decimal is simply the evaluation of the interpretation of b.

Example 4: Convert the binary number 11010 to decimal.

$$11010_2 = 0*2^0 + 1*2^1 + 0*2^2 + 1*2^3 + 1*2^4 = 26_{10}$$

Hexadecimal to Decimal Conversion

Analogous to the binary number system, the interpretation of a hexadecimal number h, which is the sequence of hexadecimal digits $h0*16^0 + \ldots + hn*16^n$, yields the decimal equivalent d of the hexadecimal number h.

Example 5: Convert the hexadecimal number $10F_{16}$ to decimal.

$$10F_{16} = F*16^0 + 0*16^1 + 1*16^2 = 271_{10}$$

Decimal to Binary Conversion

A decimal number d is converted to its binary equivalent b using the following algorithm:

Repeat until d is zero
—divide d by 2 (using integer division)
—record the remainder of the division

The sequence of all remainders obtained from the above repeated division by 2 is the desired binary number b. The remainders must be recorded from right to left, i.e. the remainder of the first division becomes the least significant bit.

Example 6: Convert the decimal number 26 to binary.

$$
\begin{array}{lll}
26 : 2 = 13 & \text{remainder } 0 \\
13 : 2 = 6 & \text{remainder } 1 \\
6 : 2 = 3 & \text{remainder } 0 \\
3 : 2 = 1 & \text{remainder } 1 \\
1 : 2 = 0 & \text{remainder } 1 \\
& \qquad\qquad 11010
\end{array}
$$

Decimal to Hexadecimal Conversion

A decimal number d may be converted to its hexadecimal equivalent h using the following algorithm:

1. repeat until d is zero
    —divide d by 16 (using integer division)
    —record the remainder of the division

2. convert all remainders to hexadecimal digits (using table F.1)

The sequence of all remainders (in hexadecimal) obtained from the above repeated division by 16 is the desired hexadecimal number h. (The remainder of the first division becomes the least significant digit.)

Example 7: Convert the decimal number 271 to binary.

$$
\begin{array}{rcl}
 & & \text{decimal} \quad \text{hexadecimal} \\
271 : 16 = 16 \quad \text{remainder} & 15 & = \quad F \\
16 : 16 = 1 \quad \text{remainder} & 0 & = \quad 0 \\
1 : 16 = 0 \quad \text{remainder} & 1 & = \quad 1 \\
\end{array}
$$

10F

Hexadecimal to Binary/Binary to Hexadecimal Conversion

The hexadecimal number system comprises 16 digits, 0 through F. To express 16 distinct combinations in the binary number system, 4 bits are necessary. When considering table F.1, it can be seen that 1 hexadecimal digit can be expressed in exactly 4 bits, i.e., $0_{16} = 0000_2$, $1_{16} = 0001_2$, ..., $F_{16} = 1111_2$. This fact is used to convert hexadecimal numbers to binary and vice versa:

> To convert a hexadecimal number h to its binary equivalent, substitute for each digit h the corresponding four binary digits, using table F.1.

Example 8: Convert $3A5_{16}$ to binary.

By substituting 0011 for 3, 1010 for A, and 0101 for 5 we obtain the binary equivalent 110100101_2. (The leading two zeros have been omitted.)

To convert a binary number b to its hexadecimal equivalent, substitute for each group of four binary digits the corresponding hexadecimal digit from table F.1. In case the number of binary digits in b is not a multiple of four, the left-most digits are padded with zeros prior to the substitution.

Example 9: Convert 110100101_2 to hexadecimal.

First, two leading zeros are attached to the number to increase the number of bits to 12, a multiple of four.

Then, by substituting 3 for 0011, A for 1010, and 5 for 0101, the hexadecimal equivalent $3A5_{16}$ is obtained.

F.2 NEGATIVE INTEGERS

To understand the principles of negative number representation, it is necessary to realize that in a computer system any number is stored as a string of n zeros and ones, where the number n is determined by the computer hardware (e.g., the size of memory words, registers, etc.). The number n imposes a restriction on the largest/smallest integer that can be represented in a particular system.

For the sake of this section we assume that any number is kept in a field comprising 8 bits. This implies that 256 (= 2 to the power of 8) combinations of zeros and ones are possible. Assuming that the number of positive and negative numbers to be represented must be the same, we conclude that, at most, 128 positive numbers (0 through + 127) and 128 negative numbers (− 0 through − 127) can be represented in 8 bits.

The following sections present three distinct schemes to map the range of 256 numbers onto the set of 256 possible bit combinations.

F.2.1 Signed Magnitude Representation

In this representation, the left-most bit of each of the 256 bit-combinations is designated as the sign-bit: 0 represents the sign " + " and 1 represents the sign " − ." The remaining 7 bits are interpreted as the absolute value, referred to as the *magnitude,* of the number being represented.

Table F.2 shows the correspondence between decimal values in the range from + 127 to − 127 and their internal representations in the three schemes presented in this section.

Negation in Signed Magnitude Representation

Negation refers to an operation which transforms a positive number to its negative equivalent or vice versa. In the signed magnitude representation the sign of a number is represented as a separate bit, thus, to perform a negation, only the sign bit needs to be complemented. Compare, for example, the numbers 1 and − 1, 2 and − 2, etc., in table F.2—each pair differs only in the left-most bit.

The signed magnitude representation is intuitively the simplest scheme to comprehend; however, it is rather difficult to implement electronic circuits to perform arithmetic operations on numbers in this representation. Consider, for example, the add and subtract operations; in either case the current sign bits and magnitudes of the operands must be compared and a sequence of decisions must be made before the actual operation may be performed. This is illustrated by the following example.

Example 10: Subtract the value 5 from the value 3 in the signed magnitude representation, i.e., 00000011 − 00000101. (The minus sign represents the subtract operation, not the sign of the operand.)

To perform this operation, the hardware circuit must first compare the absolute values of the operands. Since 5 is larger than 3, the operands must be reversed and the subtraction 5 − 3 is performed. (Note that the same scheme is followed by humans when subtracting a larger number from a smaller one in the decimal system.). Hence, the following subtraction is performed: 00000101 − 00000011.

After the subtraction, the sign bit of the result must be explicitly changed from 0 to 1 to compensate for the fact that the operands were reversed. This yields the final result, 10000010, corresponding to the value − 2.

In an attempt to simplify the algorithms for add and subtract operations, other representations for negative numbers have been developed which eliminate the comparisons necessary in the signed magnitude representation. The most common of these—the one's complement and the two's complement representations—are presented in the following sections.

F.2.2 One's Complement Representation

In this representation, positive numbers have the same form as in the signed magnitude representation. Negative numbers, on the other hand, are obtained by complementing not only the sign bit but all bits of the corresponding positive number. The operation of complementing all bits of a given number (positive or negative) is called the *one's complement*.

Negation in the One's Complement Representation

In the one's complement representation the left-most bit still indicates the sign of a number; the remaining bits, however, are not its absolute value if the number is negative. Thus, a negation cannot be performed by simply complementing the left-most bit alone; rather, the one's complement operation must be applied, i.e., all bits of the number (positive or negative) must be complemented. Table F.2 shows the range of decimal numbers from $+127$ to -127 and their one's complement equivalents.

Arithmetics in One's Complement Representation

Addition

Similar to the add operation in the decimal system, the sum of two binary numbers x and y is obtained by a bit-wise addition starting with the right-most bits of x and y. A carry, which can have only the value 0 or 1, is propagated from right to left in the same way as in a decimal addition.

For the bit-wise addition the following rules apply:

$$0 + 0 = 0 \quad \text{carry: } 0$$
$$0 + 1 = 1 \quad \text{carry: } 0$$
$$1 + 0 = 1 \quad \text{carry: } 0$$
$$1 + 1 = 0 \quad \text{carry: } 1$$

The main advantage of the one's complement representation over the signed magnitude representation is the fact that arithmetic operations always follow the same procedure, regardless of the sign of the operands. To obtain the sum of two binary numbers x and y, either of which may be positive or negative, the following steps are performed:

1. Add the two numbers x and y by applying the bit-wise addition, starting with the right-most bit and propagating the carry at each addition.
2. Add the last carry generated in the left-most position to the result obtained by the addition in step 1. (This is the carry which is shifted to the "outside" of the 8-bit word assumed in this section.)

Example 11: Add the numbers 45 and -81 in one's complement representation (assuming 8-bit words).

$$
\begin{array}{ll}
\begin{array}{r}
00101101 \\
10101110 \\
\hline
00101100 \\
11011011
\end{array}
&
\begin{array}{l}
\\
\\
\text{carry} \\
\text{result}
\end{array}
\end{array}
$$

The one's complement representation of − 81 is obtained by complementing all bits of + 81, i.e. 01010001.

The carry generated in the left-most position is zero, hence adding it to the result 11011011 does not cause any changes in the final result.

The left-most bit of the result indicates a negative value. To find its decimal equivalent, the result is complemented, which yields its positive equivalent 00100100 (36 in decimal). Thus, the result of the above add operation is − 36.

Example 12: Add the numbers − 48 and − 43 in one's complement representation.

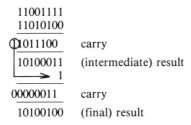

11001111	
11010100	
01011100	carry
10100011	(intermediate) result
1	
00000011	carry
10100100	(final) result

The carry generated in the left-most position is 1 and must be added to the intermediate result 10100011. This yields the final result, 10100100, which corresponds to the decimal value − 91.

Overflow

As mentioned before, because of the constraints imposed by the machine architecture, there is a limit on the largest and smallest integer that can be represented in a particular system. In this section we have assumed 8 bits to be the size of any integer.

An arithmetic operation such as add or subtract may generate a result which lies outside of the range of representable integers. Such a condition is referred to as *overflow*.

In the one's complement representation, the following simple rule is used to detect possible overflow:

If the signs of both operands are equal and the sign of the result is different, overflow has occurred.

When an overflow has occurred, the value obtained as the result is meaningless.

Example 13: Add the numbers − 126 and − 120 in one's complement.

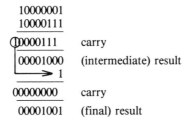

10000001	
10000111	
00000111	carry
00001000	(intermediate) result
1	
00000000	carry
00001001	(final) result

An overflow has occurred since the left-most bit of the result is 0 while the left-most bits of both operands are 1. The overflow has occurred because the expected result -246 is too small to be represented in 8 bits. Hence the value 00001001 (9 in decimal) obtained as the final result is meaningless.

Subtraction

As in decimal arithmetics, a number y may be subtracted from a number x by adding its negative equivalent $-y$ to x. Thus, in the one's complement representation, the subtract operation $x - y$ may be performed by adding the one's complement of y to x, i.e., $x - y = x + \text{complement}(y)$. This operation may be performed regardless of the sign of x and y.

Example 14: Subtract $+9$ from -3 in one's complement.

Internally, the values 9 and -3 are represented as 00001001 and 11111100, respectively. To perform the desired operation, the value 00001001 is complemented, yielding the value 11110110, and added to 11111100:

```
         11111100
         11110110
        ⓞ1111100    carry
        |11110010    (intermediate) result
        └──➤ 1
         00000000    carry
         11110011    (final) result
```

The result is the expected value -12 obtained from the subtraction $(-3)-(+9)$.

F.2.3 Two's Complement Representation

One of the problems encountered in the one's complement representation discussed previously is the fact that two distinct representations for zero, "positive" zero, 00000000, and "negative" zero, 11111111, exist. (The same is true for the signed magnitude representation where 00000000 and 10000000 represent the value zero.) Since both numbers represent the same value, electronic circuits, which perform arithmetic and comparison operations must take both representations into consideration. The two's complement representation eliminates this problem by providing only one representation for zero.

The *two's complement* of a number (positive or negative) is obtained by first performing the one's complement operation and then adding a 1 to the result.

Negation in the Two's Complement Representation

Computing the two's complement of a number x corresponds to the negation of x. Thus, to change the sign of x from positive to negative or vice versa, first the one's complement of x is obtained and then a 1 is added to the result.

Example 15: Obtain the two's complement of the value -12.

The binary equivalent of $+12$ represented in 8 bits is the number 00001100. The one's complement of 00001100 is 11110011. By adding a 1 to 11110011, the desired two's complement representation is obtained:

$$
\begin{array}{ll}
11110011 & \\
\underline{\hspace{4em}1} & \\
00000011 & \text{carry} \\
11110100 & \text{result}
\end{array}
$$

The number 11110100 represents the value -12 in two's complement.

Note that computing the two's complement of the value -12 yields the original value $+12$.

Arithmetics in Two's Complement Representation

Addition

The rules to perform an add operation in two's complement are similar to those introduced for the one's complement representation; the only distinction is the treatment of the carry generated in the left-most position. In the two's complement addition this carry is simply discarded, as opposed to being added to the result.

Example 16: Add the numbers -49 and 56 in two's complement.

$$
\begin{array}{ll}
11001111 & \\
\underline{00111000} & \\
11111000 & \text{carry} \\
00000111 & \text{result}
\end{array}
$$

The carry generated in the left-most position is discarded.

The rule to detect overflow in a two's complement addition is the same as that presented for the one's complement representation:

> If both operands have the same sign and the sign of the result is different, overflow has occurred.

Example 17: Add the numbers 64 and 65 in two's complement.

Both numbers are positive hence no complement operations are necessary:

$$
\begin{array}{ll}
01000000 & \\
\underline{01000001} & \\
01000000 & \text{carry} \\
10000001 & \text{result}
\end{array}
$$

Overflow has occurred and hence the result obtained is meaningless.

Subtraction

Analogous to the subtraction in one's complement, a number y is subtracted from a number x by adding the two's complement of y to x, regardless of the sign of either operand.

Example 18: Subtract $+9$ from -3 in two's complement.

Internally, the values 9 and -3 are represented as 00001001 and 11111101, respectively. To perform the desired operation the value 00001001 is two's-complemented, yielding the value 11110111, and then added to 11111100:

$$
\begin{array}{ll}
11111101 & \\
\underline{11110111} & \\
11111111 & \text{carry} \\
\hline
11110100 & \text{result}
\end{array}
$$

The result is the expected value -12, obtained from the subtraction $(-3) - (+9)$ in two's complement.

decimal	binary	hexadecimal
0	0	0
1	1	1
2	10	2
3	11	3
4	100	4
5	101	5
6	110	6
7	111	7
8	1000	8
9	1001	9
10	1010	A
11	1011	B
12	1100	C
13	1101	D
14	1110	E
15	1111	F
16	10000	10
17	10001	11
18	10010	12
19	10011	13
20	10100	14
21	10101	15
22	10110	16
23	10111	17
24	10000	18
25	11001	19
26	11010	1A
27	11011	1B
28	11100	1C
29	11101	1D
30	11110	1E
31	11111	1F
32	100000	20

Table F.1

decimal	signed magnitude	one's compl.	two's compl.
127	01111111	01111111	01111111
126	01111110	01111110	01111110
125	01111101	01111101	01111101
.	.	.	.
.	.	.	.
.	.	.	.
5	00000101	00000101	00000101
4	00000100	00000100	00000100
3	00000011	00000011	00000011
2	00000010	00000010	00000010
1	00000001	00000001	00000001
0	00000000	00000000	00000000
−0	10000000	11111111	−−
−1	10000001	11111110	11111111
−2	10000010	11111101	11111110
−3	10000011	11111100	11111101
−4	10000100	11111011	11111100
−5	10000101	11111010	11111011
.	.	.	.
.	.	.	.
.	.	.	.
−125	11111101	10000010	10000011
−126	11111110	10000001	10000010
−127	11111111	10000000	10000001

Table F.2

INDEX